Markers

Annual Journal of the Association for Gravestone Studies

Volume 41 • 2026

Established in 1980, *Markers* is the official journal of the Association for Gravestone Studies. Broadly interdisciplinary and multidisciplinary, the journal presents rigorous analysis and interpretation of gravestones, monuments, tombs, and cemeteries, delving into areas such as ritual and belief, economics and technology, and genealogy and conservation and especially highlighting the tangible objects—cemeteries and gravestones—that are its central focus.

Markers (ISSN 0277-8726) is published annually in the spring (Northern Hemisphere) by the University of Minnesota Press and is a benefit of membership in the Association for Gravestone Studies. For current subscription rates, please see our website: https://www.upress.umn.edu. Digital subscriptions are available online through the Project MUSE Hosted Journals Program at https://muse.jhu.edu/.

If ordering by mail, please make checks payable to the University of Minnesota Press and send to

Markers
University of Minnesota Press
111 Third Avenue South, Suite 290
Minneapolis, MN 55401-2520

Address subscription orders, changes of address, and business correspondence (including requests for permission and advertising orders) to the University of Minnesota Press, attention *Markers*.

Essays (up to 6,000 words) should be prepared according to the *Chicago Manual of Style*. *Markers* is a lavishly illustrated journal and encourages up to 20 illustrations, not including tables and charts. Authors' names should not appear on manuscripts; instead, please include a separate document with the author's name and address and the title of the article with your electronic submission. Authors should not refer to themselves in the first person in the submitted text or notes if such references would identify them; any necessary references to an author's previous work, for example, should be in the third person. All inquiries and submissions should be directed to agsmarkers@gmail.com.

Books for review should be addressed to:

Joy Giguere
Book Review Editor, *Markers*
23 South Pleasant Avenue
Dallastown, PA 17313

The Association for Gravestone Studies (AGS) was founded in 1977 for the purpose of furthering the study and preservation of gravestones. AGS is an international organization with an interest in gravemarkers of all periods and styles. Through its publications, conferences, workshops, and exhibits, AGS promotes the study of gravestones from historical and artistic perspectives, expands public awareness of the significance of historic gravemarkers, and encourages individuals and groups to record and preserve gravestones. To learn more, please visit its website, https://www.gravestonestudies.org.

Cover art: *Cypresses and road leading to the cemetery, Scutari, Constantinople, Turkey, between circa 1890 and 1900*. Library of Congress Prints and Photographs Division, LOT 13428, no. 005. Public domain. https://www.loc.gov/pictures/item/2001699428/.

MARKERS 41 • 2026

Contents

Editor's Introduction

Elisabeth L. Roark

This volume of *Markers* includes four feature articles and five book reviews, tapping into scholarship that ranges, in the feature articles, from the examination of a newly discovered nineteenth-century carver from south central Tennessee to cypresses as an indicator of graveyards in views and maps of Istanbul, Turkey. The book reviews, a recent and recurring addition to *Markers,* also investigate a variety of recent scholarship, part of our effort to inform readers of the important publications in the field. They are similarly characterized by their range, from the first scholarly English language book on Italy's monumental cemeteries to a study of Cemetery Citizens, the activists who dedicate their time to reviving cemeteries left to decay.

This is the second volume of *Markers* that is a collaboration with the University of Minnesota Press. We received positive feedback about their redesign of the journal, including the cover in color, and the opportunity for all Association for Gravestone Studies members to access digital volumes 40 and 41 of *Markers* in full color and all past volumes of the journal through Project MUSE. We hope you enjoy these new features!

Our first feature article, by Nancy Adgent, an AGS board member, "In Memory of Cader Baucom Jr., Stone Carver" introduces readers to a previously unknown carver whose gravemarkers display a talented hand through both simply inscribed stones and markers with more elaborate scenes. The latter follow the popular motifs of his time, the mid-nineteenth century, such as willows and mourner scenes. Through extensive field work, necessary when a carver has not been published before, Adgent identified over 150 stones either signed by or attributed to Baucom. Using archival and genealogical research, she crafts a full picture of both the life and work of a stone carver creating outside of the large urban centers, in rural southern middle Tennessee. Many of Baucom's carvings combine a sophisticated knowledge of design with a simplicity we might associate with fine folk art, working in both low and high relief.

Lynn Rainville undertook an equally challenging project by studying the deceased who more often than not have no gravemarkers. In "Dying Impoverished: The Funerary Rites, Gravestones, and Cemeteries of the Poor," Rainville uses the Commonwealth of Virginia as a case study to examine the treatment of the mortuary remains of the poor. Through field work and online and archival research she examined thousands of indigent burials. Rainville begins with the earliest laws for poor relief (including who was determined worthy to receive relief) and the type of care that developed, from "outdoor relief" provided by friends or neighbors to institutionalized poor farms and almshouses. Focus is on two types of burial grounds, potter's fields usually in public graveyards and paupers' cemeteries near the sites of poorhouses, using examples from across the commonwealth. Most of the burial grounds are in very poor condition and most disturbingly, markers appear to have been almost an afterthought, with only a few dozen inscribed with names, some with small stones or brass markers with numbers, and the majority indicated only by depressions in the ground. Today, a growing interest in these sites in some communities has resulted in work to locate, clean, and commemorate them.

Research on American Civil War burials has long found a place in *Markers;* particularly important are studies that identify burials lost to time. Amy L. Giroux uses a new methodology to identify the graves of Union soldiers buried in the St. Francis Barracks Post Cemetery in St. Augustine, Florida. She convincingly argues that the soldiers, when they received their standard military gravestones in 1905, had been long forgotten and were marked mistakenly as unknowns of the Indian Wars of 1842. In "Restoring Their Honor: Image Forensics Identifies Lost Graves of Union Soldiers," Giroux uses a stereogram taken around 1865, which shows decaying wooden markers in the cemetery. Nine of the markers have partially discernable text, six of which are made more visible to us by augmenting the text in the illustrations in the article. Establishing their regiment and comparing the names with a list of the deceased in the cemetery made two years later, Giroux was able to reconnect their names with their markers and prove that they had died during the Civil War. She was then able to determine, using government records, that at least ninety soldiers died in St. Augustine; sixty are buried in the cemetery under the mis-inscribed markers.

F. İkbal Sezen Polat's article, "'A Cypress Tree for Each Dead': The Unique Gravemarker in Istanbul's Skyline and Visual Urban Representations," introduces us to the many implications of cypress trees in Turkish culture, as a symbol, a literary device, a cultural icon, and most importantly for our interests, as a representation of Muslim cemeteries. In a fascinating array of maps and views that date from the sixteenth to the twentieth centuries, she traces the increasing visual power of cypresses, which present a vertical element that marks the cemeteries and without which, due to their horizontal orientation, they would lack prominence. Polat investigates cypresses in the graveyards from two perspectives: cypresses as representations of human beings, both the body and soul, and cypresses as near-architectural manifestations, paralleling other vertical elements in the city skyline such as minarets and towers. She draws both strands together to argue that cypresses serve a dual purpose in these images, as architectural markers and symbols of human life as a presence that endures death.

Markers is currently indexed in the *Bibliography of the History of Art, America: History and Life, Historical Abstracts,* and the *MLA International Bibliography.* In partnership with the University of Massachusetts Amherst Special Collections Library, the Association for Gravestone Studies archives many early issues of *Markers,* available on the University of Massachusetts Amherst Libraries website for free viewing and downloading. As noted, this issue, and volumes from recent and past years now appear on Project MUSE and are available to AGS members. Nonmembers may purchase individual articles from Project MUSE or join AGS to have full access. See the Membership page on the AGS website at *https://www.gravestonestudies.org/*. As editor, I welcome queries about appropriate content for *Markers* before article submission. Prospective authors should read the *Markers* page on the AGS website and follow the "Style Guide" and "Notes for Contributors" (links appear at the bottom of the page) prior to submitting a manuscript. Please send questions, comments, and submissions to agsmarkers@gmail.com. Inquiries about books to be considered for review should be sent to Joy Giguere, at jmg66@psu.edu.

Elisabeth L. (Beth) Roark is editor of *Markers* and a professor of art history and museum studies at Chatham University. She received an MA and PhD from the University of Pittsburgh and a BA from Allegheny

College where she was elected to Phi Beta Kappa. Other awards include a Mellon Fellowship and a Smithsonian Pre-Doctoral Fellowship. Beth has published and presented widely on colonial and nineteenth-century American art, including articles in *Markers, Prospects, American Art, Italian American Review, Maryland Historical Magazine, Nineteenth-Century Art Worldwide,* the *Gazette des Beaux-Arts,* and the book *Artists of Colonial America.* Current research interests include Italian-made sculpture found in America's nineteenth-century rural cemeteries and the funerary sculpture of George Grey Barnard.

In Memoriam

James Stevens Curl

The architectural historian Dr. James Stevens Curl died in November 2025 at the age of eighty-eight.

An Ulsterman, he trained as an architect at what was then the Oxford School of Architecture, and then as a town planner, before becoming an architectural historian, working in the 1970s for the Survey of London. His PhD at University College, London, was on the Victorian architect Henry Roberts, known for his model housing for the working classes.

He was an extraordinarily prolific writer of scholarly works, including the useful *Oxford Dictionary of Architecture* (Oxford University Press, 1999, second edition 2006) and the *Art and Architecture of Freemasonry* (Batsford, London, 1991).

He was a man of forceful views and personality, and not one to hide his light under a bushel. He had a particular hatred of the Modern Movement which he anathematised in one of his last books, *Making Distopia* (Oxford University Press, 2018).

However, his importance to readers of this journal is that he was (extraordinarily) the first person in the British Isles to give full, scholarly attention to cemeteries and the gravemarkers they contain. His most notable publication on the subject was *Kensal Green Cemetery: The Origins and Development of the General Cemetery of All Souls, Kensal Gren, London, 1824-2001* (Phillimore, Chichester, 2001), about one of the big London cemeteries. He was editor and also wrote most of the articles; it remains a model for such studies.

Jonathan Kewley

Frontispiece. Hannah Patterson, 1847, Old Mars Hill Cemetery, Cornersville. Typical cemetery mourner scene motif. Photograph by the author.

In Memory of Cader Baucom Jr., Stone Carver

Nancy Adgent

About halfway between Nashville and the Alabama state line in Marshall County, Tennessee, stands a tombstone unusual for this area and time period—one emblazoned in the lower left with a bold carver signature, "C. Baucom." It is on a rather ordinary tablet headstone with an 1857 death date in the Old Mars Hill Presbyterian Church graveyard established in 1825, one of the oldest burial grounds in the area (Figure 1). In rural Middle Tennessee during the pioneer period (1790s–1830s), grave markers for people not among the wealthy elite were typically rough field stones with no inscription, dressed stone cairns, or unembellished sandstone or limestone tablets. During a decade or so exploring Tennessee graveyards, I had seen signatures of only three other individual carvers, one in Middle Tennessee dated in the 1870s and two in East Tennessee with dates in the 1880s. Though this marker had no decoration, the inscription was a combination of lovely cursive script for "In Memory Of" and "Was Born" with the remainder in simple block lettering imperfectly spaced. Surely a carver with such elegant phrasing who signed a simple stone would have signed other, more elaborate creations.[1]

Because no studies of Tennessee carvers were to be found, field research had to be the primary means of discovering additional Baucom works. In the same graveyard as the initial stone, there are at least ten others with similar characteristics. Most are unadorned; however, a few have cemetery mourner motifs such as the ones for Elizabeth Ross (1837), Hannah Patterson (1847) (Figure 2), and Nancy Davis (1856). To date, I have found twenty Baucom signed markers plus six additional ones probated—an astonishing number considering that his work has been

Figure 1. Samuel Kincaid, 1857, Old Mars Hill Cemetery, Cornersville. Signed "C. Baucom." Photograph by the author.

Figure 2. Hannah Patterson, 1847, Old Mars Hill Cemetery, Cornersville. Typical cemetery mourner scene motif. Photograph by the author.

completely unstudied. At least 138 more markers with similar characteristics are attributable to Baucom. Some elements are distinctive: *8*s that look like one small *o* atop another; *c*s that are almost *g*s; *A*s with a low cross bar; *7*s that are unusually wide at the base; *1*s that look like capital *I*s; use of "th" after days; periods after the surname and years; cursive "In Memory Of," "Who," and "Died" (Figure 3). Some have a graveyard mourner motif, others are undecorated tablets, one is a table tomb, two are chest tombs, four are linked pedestal groupings, and several are Baucom's signature obelisk with high relief weeping willow. Except a few for family members, all are within a fifty-mile range of Pulaski, Giles County, Tennessee. Even though his lettering for names and dates is at times a bit uneven and unremarkable, the beautiful script on the standard (not specific to the deceased) sections of the stones and the range of decorative motifs and marker styles signify a master craftsman operating in a place and period when few others could compete artistically.[2]

Figure 3. Mary Elizabeth Rhodes, 1843, Beechwood Cemetery, Cornersville. This tablet shows Baucom's usual lettering style. Photograph by the author.

Other than an occasional brief notation in National Register nominations and in cemetery-produced pamphlets, nineteenth-century Tennessee gravestone carvers have not been identified and studied. Even the National Register nomination for Maplewood Cemetery, Pulaski, where several Baucom markers stand, does not mention his name although his willows on obelisks are noted. Since at least the beginning of the twentieth century, researchers have investigated carvers and motifs, and during the fifty or so years after the 1927 publication of Harriette Merrifield Forbes's *Gravestones of Early New England and the Men Who Made Them, 1653–1800,* scholars greatly expanded the scope of gravestone investigations. Nevertheless, most studies focused on New England and the Mid-Atlantic states in the seventeenth and eighteenth centuries with little attention paid to the South and later periods. Near the turn of the twenty-first century and over the next two decades, Ralph Bailey, Terry Jordan-Bychkov, Ruth Little, and Daniel Patterson delved into this neglected region and the nineteenth century, primarily in the Carolinas, Arkansas, and Texas. Such a long-neglected aspect of Tennessee history and gravestone research deserves attention, and beginning with C. Baucom is a serendipitous choice.[3]

BAUCOM FAMILY (1800–1857)

Genealogical research shed some light on this noteworthy carver's influences and client connections. Cader Baucom Jr., the youngest of eight children, was born April 13, 1819, to Cader Baucom Sr. (1775–1852) and Susanna Fowler Baucom (1777–1840) who married on July 31, 1797. In 1800, the family is shown in the Hillsborough, Wake County, North Carolina, census. The Baucom family evidently moved to Tennessee around 1812 because the last two children were born in the state in 1813 and 1819. In the 1820 and 1830 censuses, the senior Baucom was enumerated in rural Williamson County as a farmer. The Baucoms were undoubtedly among the numerous Scots-Irish Presbyterians who made their way from western North Carolina into Middle Tennessee after the Revolutionary War, many claiming land grants for their service. Lending credence to this assumption are attributed Baucom markers for Rev. James Hall, cofounder of several Presbyterian churches in Tennessee; a brother-in-law who was a Presbyterian minister; and several of Baucom's markers in at least four historically Presbyterian cemeteries—Old Mars Hill, New Hope, First Presbyterian, and Brick Church.[4]

The family was not listed in the 1840 census. Baucom Jr.'s mother, Susanna, had died in March which could have caused the remaining household consisting of father and youngest son to dismantle. Susanna is buried in a small Wilson family graveyard near Eagleville, Rutherford County. With his older brothers married and living in other counties, young Cader probably needed to support himself as soon as he could and he may have moved to live with relatives or an employer even before his mother's death. One possibility is that he lived with his sister Nancy's family. She married Presbyterian minister Rev. Josiah F. Wilson on July 28, 1831, in Williamson County, and they lived in adjoining Marshall County in 1840 and 1850. In 1840, their household included a male aged fifteen to nineteen when their oldest child would have been no more than nine years old, which indicates that Baucum Jr. may have lived there for the first few years of his working life. In November 1841, he married Cynthia Anna Elizabeth Busby in Lawrence County, about sixty miles from his parents' 1830 residence and adjoining Giles County where his earliest signed marker stands.[5]

At least by May 1849, Baucom Jr. and family were living in Pulaski, Giles County, Tennessee, where he was listed as a stone cutter in the 1850 census. His sister, Susan, and her husband, William Peach, were also in Pulaski in 1850 and Peach's occupation was also stone cutter. By that time, Baucom Sr. was living with his daughter, Charlotte Sutton, and her family in Williamson County. The elder Baucom died in adjacent Rutherford County, where in April 1852 the county court ordered that "T. L. Hendrix be allowed the sum of Five dollars for a coffin furnished by him to bury Cader Baucum dec'd a pauper."[6] Even though he had recently lived with the Suttons and they appeared to have had resources for his burial, I could find no documentation of a gravesite. Baucom Jr.'s brother Wilson died before 1850, and brothers John and Willis were living about 150–200 miles northwest of Williamson and Rutherford Counties. The lack of a marker for the father of a successful gravestone carver seems a bit odd. One possibility is that the two were estranged; however, it is also possible that Baucom Jr. was too engulfed in his own life changes and grief to attend to his father's burial. About six months after giving birth, his wife, "Mrs. S. A. E. Baucom Died in the triumph of Religion,

December 31st 1852." She had advertised in September a change of location for her dress making and millinery business, so her death must have been unexpected. In the year following Cynthia's death, Baucom married Mary E. White. Both the 1850 and 1860 censuses note that all his school age children, including the girls, were attending school, following the Presbyterian tradition of valuing education. Baucom's family life centered around his nuclear family and his sister Susan Peach's family to whom he lived nearby for most of his professional life.[7]

GENESIS OF A STONE CARVER

As pioneers moved west, so did stone carvers, seeking less competition and new clientele. Although the origin of Baucom's carving skill is speculative, a Williamson County neighbor, Joe White, may have trained Baucom. White was not shown in the 1840 census, but in the 1850 census, he was shown to be living near Baucom Sr. and the Wilsons and Suttons who married into the Baucom family. About ten years older than Baucom Jr., White would have been experienced enough with adequate demand in the late 1830s and early 1840s to have needed an apprentice. Another possibility is that Baucom was trained by his brother-in-law, William Peach, who was also ten years or so older and came from an extended family with at least four other stone craftsmen; however, Baucom and Peach were not listed near each other until the 1850 census when Baucom had already been in business for about ten years. Susan Baucom and William Peach married in July 1833 in Williamson County. Initially, Peach was likely working with relatives who were stone masons employed to construct the State Capitol (1845–1859) and other major buildings during the city's boom from the 1820s through 1850s. No stones signed by White or Peach have been found, which precludes comparison of lettering styles or even confirming that they actually carved gravestones. If Peach trained Baucom, it seems the student surpassed the teacher.[8]

The earliest Baucom signed stone is for the 1833 death of Evander Gordon in Brick Church Cemetery (Presbyterian), Giles County, about fifty miles from Baucom's domicile three years earlier (Figure 4). While the unadorned bedstead style tablet shaping is competent, the lettering workmanship is amateur and lacks the characteristics of Baucom's later

Figure 4. Evander Gordon, 1833, Brick Church Cemetery, Giles County. Baucom's earliest signed marker reflects his inexperienced lettering and spacing. Photograph by the author.

work. It is feasible that he carved it at age fourteen since it was not uncommon during that time period for young males to apprentice while still teenagers. It does seem a bit unlikely, however, that Baucom or his employer would have had a client so far away when horse and wagon would have been the only viable mode of transportation; therefore, Baucom was probably already living in the Brick Church area (near the Giles/Marshall County border) when he carved the Gordon stone. Five stones attributed to Baucom and two he signed are for decedents in the 1820s–30s, and all were in Giles County, including the portion of Marshall County that was part of Giles during Baucom's lifetime. All could, of course, have been carved much later than the death dates. May Richardson's 1822 marker most certainly was not carved when Baucom was three years old! Until Baucom launched his own shop, he likely used his master's tools and lettering style and may have experimented while learning his craft, either of which would account for his few early stones differing from his later ones. Another possibility is that Baucom lettered the Gordon marker and apprentices or Peach carved names and dates on later stones.

AN ESTABLISHED STONE CARVER (1841–1857), PULASKI, GILES COUNTY, TENNESSEE

When Baucom started his own business is uncertain. Traditionally, before marrying, a young man would have had a reliable income, thus Baucom must have established himself prior to 1841. In 1844, the court allowed Baucom to take ten-year-old orphan Mary Coker as an apprentice, so he would been considered a reputable, financially responsible citizen at that time. Marriage and family gave Baucom an incentive to significantly increase his output from the seven stones dated prior to 1840. For death dates in the 1840s, there are seven signed, two others probated, and thirty-five attributed markers.[9]

Lettering was mostly uniform throughout Baucom's career with only minor exceptions when he was learning his craft. The consistent defining element on the vast majority of his markers is the odd *8*. Generally, Baucom used all capital block letters for the person's name and dates with additional text a combination of upper and lower case. Simple tablets for cousins of his sister-in-law, Mary M. Wilson (1835) (Figure 5), and James D. M. Wilson (1842) show his typical *8* and illustrate his progression toward more ornamental script in the "daughter of" and "son of" lines. As Baucom's carving skill matured, his lettering became more pleasingly spaced, and he began using an elegant cursive script for "In Memory Of," "Born," and "Died" as seen in the 1843 Rhodes stone (Figure 3). Although Baucom incised most letters, frequently he carved the name on his decorated stones in low relief against a stippled background and sometimes used the same technique within a curved banner or rectangular plate for "In Memory Of" as in Hannah Patterson's 1847 marker (Figure 2).

As he gained experience, Baucom began producing ornamented stones. By the 1840s, markers on rural Middle Tennessee burials of farmers and merchants were transitioning to professionally carved and decorated markers. The Baucom signed marker for Sarah H. Potter (1849) in Old Graveyard Memorial Park, Pulaski, is one of his most elaborate examples of the shift in tombstone tastes and his emerging artistic talent (Figure 6). A weeping willow trunk in low relief frames each side of the tablet culminating in branches overhanging a cemetery mourner scene of three women in bonnets and a man to the left of a central pedestal with obelisk topped by a bird holding an olive branch in its beak. On the right side of

Figure 5. Mary M. Wilson, 1835, Moses-Wilson Cemetery, Chapel Hill. Baucom's transition from all block lettering to some cursive and italic. Photograph by the author.

the obelisk, there are three men in top hats and a lamb in the lower right corner. "Sacred To the Memory" letters are all capitals in low relief with the latter three words inside a curved banner. "Wife of," "Died," *8*, *7*, and *th* are in Baucom's typical style. Potter's stone also has the triple diamond line between sections, another occasional characteristic of his work. The mourners on the left may represent surviving family members while the men on the right may be pallbearers. As a symbol of the soul, the dove with an olive branch indicates that the deceased is at peace with God. Some may interpret the dove as the messenger of the Holy Spirit bringing peace to the mourners.[10] The cemetery mourner motif occurs on fourteen of Baucom's markers, four of which are signed. The earliest one (Elizabeth Ross) has an 1837 death date and is in the same cemetery as the Samuel Kincaid stone (Figure 1) where there are at least two other mourner tablets. Baucom's cemetery mourner markers extend through the 1850s and differ from each other slightly. For example, the 1847 stone for Hannah Patterson (Figure 2) has an obelisk as the first marker in the cemetery mourner motif rather than a tablet as on the 1856 Davis marker (Figure 7). Lucinda Scales' 1845 headstone in New Hope Cemetery, Cornersville, has a church in the lower right of the cemetery motif but no mourners (Figure 8). Scales' inscription

Figure 6. Sarah H. Potter, 1849, Old Graveyard Memorial Park, Pulaski. A Baucom signed cemetery mourner scene. Photograph by the author.

Figure 7. Nancy Davis, 1856, Old Mars Hill Cemetery, Cornersville. Cemetery mourner motif on pedestal for fallen obelisk with arched hood over rosette knobs on base. Photograph by the author.

Figure 8. Lucinda Scales, 1845, New Hope Cemetery, Cornersville. Motif has church in lower right corner. Photograph by the author.

notes that she was a member of the Baptist Church, a scene that appears customized for her. All have the stippled background; some have a few words in bas relief within curved banners. To date, I have not found this cemetery mourner motif on Middle Tennessee markers with lettering characteristics other than Baucom's, thus I believe this form was in his exclusive repertoire of gravestones.

Some may question whether the cemetery mourner motif tablets were purchased with the scenes and fancy script already engraved, perhaps from a Nashville or other large city dealer. If that were the case, there should be some cemetery mourner markers with lettering different from Baucom's and signatures of other carvers, which is not the case. Baucom's other markers—obelisks and pedestals—have the same script he used on undecorated tablets and mourner scenes. Baucom may have even carved his own standard ("Died," "Was Born," etc.), cursive lettering on tablets during slack times to have stock readily available when the need arose. Employees or apprentices could have then done the block cutting for names and dates after the stone was ordered. The cemetery mourner scene motif is not unique to Baucom, but his execution is different from others in that it frequently combines one or more mourners with the graveyard tableau. Slate examples depicting tombstones below a willow minus mourners exist in Readfield and Fayette, Maine, both dated in the 1840s, and marble ones in Charleston, South Carolina, in the 1850s and 60s. A few others in various states (as early as 1817 in Plymouth, Massachusetts, and as late as 1850s in Elizabeth, New Jersey) have a mourner figure leaning on a pedestal or obelisk under a willow but do not depict other tombstones, thus the more extensive cemetery scene combining mourner(s) and willow(s) with a few tombstones appears to have been a Baucom innovation.[11]

During the 1840s, Baucom developed an unusual multiple-linked pedestal configuration, including the signed quadruple one in the First Presbyterian Church Cemetery, Fayetteville, for four members of the James Russell family who died 1842, 1845, and 1847 (Figure 9). Adjacent to the Russell plot is a similar double pedestal marker for General T. A. Owen (1855) and daughter, Mary (1854). Another double linked pedestal with Baucom's trademark script and *8* is in Beechwood Cemetery, Cornersville. For two Burgess children (1853, 1856), each pedestal is topped with a full relief lamb (Figure 10). All three groupings have Baucom's characteristic lettering and the Russell marker also has a separator line with three diamonds. Similar linked pedestals with lettering different from Baucom's are absent from other area cemeteries. This type appears to be another Baucom exclusive.

By 1850, Baucom had debuted a bold, unique, high relief weeping willow design, mostly on obelisks, as shown on the marker for Mary Ewing (1853), Brick Church Cemetery, Giles County (Figure 11). Among a plethora of obelisks, his bold willow for Judeth Burch (1855) commands the most attention in a section of Maplewood Cemetery, Pulaski (Figure 12). It is signed at the base of the obelisk shaft rather than on the pedestal, positively identifying Baucom as the willow carver. The earliest signed marker of this style is for Harriet Perkins (1850) in Maplewood Cemetery, Pulaski, and the earliest attributed one is for Melissa Massey (1848) in Beechwood Cemetery, Cornersville. Ewing's and Massey's have the same "To the Memory of" banner as on Potter's signed tablet (Figure 6). The odd protruding rosette knobs under arched hoods on the Davis marker above the inscribed pedestal that once supported its obelisk differ from most pedestal to obelisk transitions and proved to

Figure 9. Russell family, 1842–47, First Presbyterian Church Cemetery, Fayetteville. Linked pedestals. Photograph by the author.

Figure 10. Burgess children, 1853, 1856, Beechwood Cemetery, Cornersville. Full relief lambs facing each other. Photograph by author.

Figure 11. Mary J. Ewing, 1853, Brick Church Cemetery, Giles County. Baucom's signature deep relief willow. Photograph by the author.

Figure 12. Judeth M. Burch, 1855, Maplewood Cemetery, Pulaski. Baucom's willow on obelisk sets his work apart from a group of ordinary obelisks. Photograph by the author.

be another trait on some Baucom obelisk pedestals (Figure 7). Thus far, four signed, raised willows plus three signed with other ornamentation are among the thirty-one Baucom obelisks. Sixteen obelisks have the willow motif and fifteen have other designs, a few of which are executed in marble rather than his usual sandstone. One of the marbles reflects the pinnacle of Baucom's craft. It combines a triple, linked pedestal form with the willow on obelisk design—for the McKissack family (1842, 1843, 1855) in Spring Hill Cemetery, Spring Hill (Figures 13 and 14). Rather than being in deep relief, Baucom's marble willows were finely executed bas relief trees within a recessed circle, oval, or rectangle, which better protected the decorative element from damage. Examples include the McKissacks', John F. McClelland's 1859 Masonic and willow obelisk (Figure 15), and John Edwards's 1860 tablet willow (Figure 16). Though these three are unsigned, the style and lettering are identical to Baucom's other stones, and the McKissack triple pedestal base duplicates the Russell family group, so these can be attributed even though the willows differ slightly in thickness of root and shape of the willow branches. The tablet for John White (1857) has a plump willow that is decidedly different from Baucom's usual representation and could have been purchased with the motif already carved (Figure 17). Since it has Baucom's characteristic lettering, he or his shop at least cut the text. A similar thick willow within a cemetery motif, and his trademark "Died" script are on the tablet for Baucom's nephew, John R. Baucom (1859) which lends credence to the plump willows being Baucom's. All but one of Baucom's willows produced after 1857 have thicker branches than his earlier willows though not quite as robust as the ones for White and nephew John. Perhaps when Baucom moved his operation to Shelbyville in 1858 and began working primarily in marble, the appearance of willows necessarily changed, or he could have discovered the relative ease of producing more lush branches in a softer material.[12]

Though Baucom was far from the only carver who favored weeping willows, his were unique. Willows and willows with urns were popular motifs from circa 1800 through most of the nineteenth century and are ubiquitous in cemeteries across the eastern United States. W. Douglas Hartley identified Henry Cross as the carver of stylized willows on sandstone in south central Indiana in the 1840s and 1850s. Duval and Rigby identified others carved by John Strickler in Fairfield County and by an

Figure 13. William McKissack family, 1855, Spring Hill Cemetery, Spring Hill. The pinnacle of Baucom's work combining willow on marble obelisk with linked pedestals. Photograph by the author.

Figure 14. McKissack obelisk, 1855, Spring Hill Cemetery, Spring Hill. Willow detail. Photograph by the author.

Figure 15. John F. McClelland, 1859, New Hope Cemetery, Cornersville. Marble willow and Masonic square and compasses on obelisk. Photograph by the author.

Figure 16. John Edwards, 1860, Beechwood Cemetery, Cornersville. Willow with thicker branches on marble tablet. Photograph by the author.

Figure 17. John White, 1857, Beechwood Cemetery, Cornersville. Plump willow. Photograph by the author.

unknown carver in Delaware County, Ohio. Of course, many tablets, particularly marble, have recessed willows, some low relief and others high relief. Fine examples stand in German cemeteries in the Doylestown, Pennsylvania, area with death dates in the 1840s–60s. Another nice willow for Lucy Savage (1859) by Cayton & Wolfe is pictured in Ruth Little's book. These were concurrent with Baucom's work, so would not have been models for him even if he had seen them. Two high relief willows in Baucom's general vicinity are in Alexander Cemetery, Theta (Virginia McMeen, 1851), and Greenwood Cemetery, Columbia (Rachel Pickard, 1854); and at least one other obelisk with recessed, low relief willow exists locally (Daniel German, 1858) in Rest Haven Cemetery, Franklin. These three do not appear to be Baucom's work as the lettering is very different, the willow branches are not tiered, and the willow trunks are not exposed almost to the top. Countrywide, other raised motifs appear in the middle of obelisks—flags, wreaths, Masonic symbols, angels, torches, guns, but not a high relief willow like Baucom's. Thus far, no evidence indicates that he traveled beyond Middle Tennessee, and similar willows in this region with lettering different from Baucom's have not been found. Baucom's execution of the willow typically projecting from an obelisk is a departure from the usual depiction of the tree and is a style not duplicated elsewhere.[13]

Baucom was versatile, carving a few markers with motifs found on only one or two of his stones and producing a variety of forms. For example, his first wife's marker in Old Graveyard Memorial Park, Pulaski, was one of his more intricate works with flowers carved in deep relief on the truncated obelisk. Unfortunately, the marble has deteriorated to the point that the flowers are barely discernable and inscriptions on the face and side are only partially legible. Cynthia's death in December 1852 was a blow that impacted Baucom's production.[14] For 1853, I have located only one signed marker and six attributed, compared with two signed and thirteen attributed in 1854. Between 1850 and 1860 he signed ten markers; ninety-one more can be attributed to him during that period. By 1855, Baucom was experimenting with other motifs, such as the man and descending bird on an obelisk for Thomas Knight, Maplewood Cemetery, Pulaski (Figure 18); the full relief lambs facing each other for the two Burgess children (1853 and 1856) (Figure 10); the oak leaf garland and heart for Martha Jane Hunt Nance (1858) (Figure 19); and a bas relief

Figure 18. Thomas Knight, 1855, Maplewood Cemetery, Pulaski. Descending dove over male figure. Photograph by the author.

Figure 19. Martha Jane Hunt Nance, 1858, Beechwood Cemetery, Cornersville. Oak leaf swag encircling heart. Photograph by the author.

draped urn on the obelisk for Margaret Williams (1854), in Old Graveyard Memorial Park, Pulaski. In addition to erecting several obelisks and a few linked pedestals, he made at least one table tomb (Nancy Hibits, 1850), and two chest tombs (Joseph Nance, 1847, and Dr. Peter Martin, 1854). Nevertheless, throughout his career, Baucom continued to make unadorned tablets, thus catering to customers of diverse economic levels and artistic tastes.

COMPETITION (1841–1857), PULASKI, GILES COUNTY, TENNESSEE

In 1850, Baucom was one of only 151 stone cutters in Tennessee, and one of 14,076 in the entire United States and its territories. For comparison, the similar size states of Ohio and Pennsylvania had 1,453 and 2,114, respectively. The tiny, long-settled state of Rhode Island had 297. Admitted to statehood only four years before Tennessee, Kentucky had 226 cutters, and Indiana, admitted twenty years after Tennessee, was home to 248 cutters. Judging by the 1850 Giles County census, stone cutter was a less common occupation than almost anything else, including "easy virtue"! It was shown in about the same numbers as druggist, watch maker, peddler, butcher, artist, banker, tinner, gardener, dentist, gin maker, engineer; however, it occurred less often than physician, lawyer, teacher, harness maker, shoemaker, saddler, merchant, mechanic, weaver, and miller in an age when the major occupations were farmer, overseer, laborer, and domestic.[15]

Baucom and his wife certainly had the potential for reliable and above average household income. As entrepreneurs, they controlled their own fortunes, to some extent, and were not dependent on the whims of nature as were farmers. The 1850 census lists Baucom's occupation as stone cutter with real estate valued at $1,200. Included in the household are two unrelated people: Columbus Pearce, age nineteen, stonecutter, and Daniel Ferguson, age eighteen, blacksmith. The 1850 slave census shows three enslaved people in his household: two males ages twenty-four and twenty-two, and one female age twenty-one. According to deeds in the 1850s, he bought four enslaved Black people, sold two women, and hired three men. Most likely the females were household help, while the males provided labor in the stone yard. Baucom's real estate value is only slightly lower than those of nearby physicians and a lawyer. Twenty houses away, Baucom's sister Susan and her stone cutter husband, William Peach, age forty-one, resided. Peach's real estate is valued at $550, and six children ranging from age fifteen to two are listed. Because Peach lived near Baucom from at least 1850 onward, he likely worked as a partner. The only other stone cutter in the town, Andrew L. Crow, age forty-six, had real estate valued at $1,000. The 1850 Industrial census shows Baucom and Crow as the only two stone cutters in the county. Baucom employed seven men at an average monthly cost of $52 and annually used 15,000 feet of "tomb stone and building mat." valued at $2,200, whereas Crow hired only two men, used one-tenth of the amount of stone, and that was "dressed stone for houses." Thus, even though Baucom was about a decade younger than the other two cutters, it seems he was the actual tombstone carver and had the more profitable business.[16]

As early as October 1851, Baucom was advertising in the *Pulaski Gazette*, even offering to take "country produce" as payment. Though it could have been an act of desperation, it was more likely an innovative, pragmatic marketing concept. It certainly set him apart from his peers, and the fact that he could afford to advertise speaks against the idea of despair. Another argument against desperation is his wife's dressmaking and millinery business, also advertised in the *Pulaski Gazette*—an unusual situation for a two-income household in that time period. Evidently Baucom's work was held in high regard, and he had prominent advocates. His references in the ad were Andrew M. Ballentine, farmer and dry goods store proprietor; Thomas Martin, prominent merchant, banker, and railroad president; and Albert Moore, editor of the *Pulaski Gazette*. (Baucom's Bible notes that two of his children were named for Martin and his daughter.) In a letter to the editor of the *Pulaski Citizen* published June 8, 1866, the mocking author of "Alvin Replies to Concilium" opined: "He says we haint got no painters nor sculptors here! . . . And whar'll he find such sculptur as the birds and flowers and tombstone cut by Crow and Woodring, and used to be cut by Cader Baucum in your city?"[17]

In the mid and late 1850s, as roads improved and railroads expanded, rural towns such as Pulaski gained easier and cheaper access to larger and more expensive gravemarkers from suppliers in Nashville and beyond.

While very wealthy families such as the Polks in adjacent Maury County ordered their markers from R. E. Launitz in New York, well-to-do Pulaski families such as Robert H. Watkins (1855) turned to Sloan & Mitchell of Nashville. A January 1854 advertisement for Nashville Steam Marble Works, owned by James Sloan, touted "a large assortment of Monuments, Tombs, Baptismal Founts, urns, Vases, Garden Figures, Grave Stones, etc. carved and lettered to order" with marble from Italy, Egypt, East Tennessee, and elsewhere in the United States. Markers from more distant monument companies began appearing in Maplewood Cemetery, Pulaski's primary burial ground, one of which was for Baucom's reference, Andrew M. Ballantine (1863). His marker is a large, lavishly embellished marble Gothic style temple form pedestal topped with an angel sculpture from T. White & Son, Cincinnati. Transportation advances led to a gradual decline in tombstones made from locally sourced, poor-quality sandstone and limestone and to the demise of individual stone carvers not affiliated with large monument companies.[18]

BAUCOM'S LAST DECADE: TUMULTUOUS TIMES (1858–1867), SHELBYVILLE AND NASHVILLE

Despite his apparent success, by October 1858, Baucom had sold his Pulaski house, office, and stone yard, and moved to Shelbyville, about fifty miles northeast of Pulaski. One of his signed stones with a death date of November 1858 has "Shelbyville" inscribed beneath "C. Baucum & Co."—a more elaborate signature than on his earlier markers (Figure 20). In the 1860 census, the family was shown in Shelbyville with no real estate but with personal property valued at $400. The 1860 slave census shows three enslaved people in his household—one male, age sixty-five; one female, age sixty; and one female, age sixteen. He is again in a neighborhood with an attorney, physician, stable keeper, and tailor. The Peach family was in the same county in 1860 as well, and their twenty-three-year-old son, Lewis, is listed as a stone cutter, perhaps part of the Baucom "company" referenced in the Nance tombstone signature.[19]

Why would Baucom have left what appeared to be a successful business in Pulaski? He could have been pressured by an increasing number of competitors in Giles County (five in 1860 versus one in 1850) to seek

Figure 20. Martha Jane Hunt Nance, 1858, Beechwood Cemetery, Cornersville. Base with more elaborate signature "C. Baucum & Co., Shelbyville, Tenn." Photograph by the author.

a new market for his talents. Based on the 1858 Nance stone, perhaps he purchased the equipment of a steam or water-powered stone business based in Shelbyville. Or, he may have foreseen the coming conflict and moved to Shelbyville, known as "Little Boston," to be among its majority Unionist sympathizers. As a slave owner, he was not, however, an abolitionist. His reasons for moving are almost impossible to determine nearly two centuries later.[20]

One argument in favor of his Unionist beliefs is that he moved to Nashville sometime between 1860 and 1864, probably around the time the city surrendered to the Union Army on February 24, 1862, and established its Department of the Cumberland Headquarters. He very likely was in Nashville before Confederates occupied Shelbyville in March 1863. Tennessee was almost evenly divided between Confederate and Union sympathizers, primarily because East and much of Middle Tennessee consisted of small, subsistence farms with fewer slaves than West Tennessee which had a cotton-growing plantation economy dependent on the labor of enslaved people. Initially Tennesseans voted down secession;

however, after the fall of Fort Sumter and Lincoln's call for the state to furnish a militia, secession fever invaded the state. Droves of young men joined the rebel army by summer 1861, and many Unionists fled North, some to join Federal forces in other states. At about age forty-three when the first Confederate draft was enacted in April 1862, Baucom would have been exempt; however, when the 1864 Conscription Act changed the limit to age fifty, he could have been drafted had he still been living in rebel-held territory instead of within Union-occupied Nashville, where he was also safe from Lincoln's draft, which was capped at age thirty-five for married men. He is not listed as a Civil War soldier according to the Civil War Soldiers and Sailors Database website and his source of income and activities during the war are speculative.[21]

Moving a family during war would have been a harrowing undertaking regardless of any expected improvement in circumstances. With five girls and two boys under the age of eighteen in 1862, Baucom was pragmatic enough to realize that his family would be safer inside Union lines, and that he could remain gainfully employed in a city with a thriving economy based on supporting a large army in an important transportation hub. Years earlier, being a self-employed tradesman not dependent on Mother Nature was an advantage; now, having no land on which to grow food, and customers with no funds to pay for tombstones, operating a nonessential business was a distinct disadvantage. Food, schools, medical facilities, law enforcement, employment—necessities sorely lacking in war-torn countryside—were all available in occupied Nashville. After April 1863, the town included numerous Unionist refugees from East and Middle Tennessee as well as formerly enslaved people who had escaped farms in the region, all of whom were somewhat protected by the occupying Union Army. Some staunch secessionists had fled to the Deep South or been imprisoned, especially after residents of Nashville were required to take a loyalty oath to the Union. Whatever Baucom's reasons, the move was almost certainly beneficial for his family.[22]

Exactly how the Baucom family survived during the war is undetermined, though it is doubtful that they relied on income from his stone carving. Despite the transit of thousands of dead and dying soldiers to and through Nashville, circumstances meant their graves were marked with temporary wooden markers. By war's end, over 12,000 Union and Confederate dead had been buried in the "soldiers" section of Nashville

City Cemetery and in what became Nashville's National Cemetery. Union graves were not marked with government supplied marble headstones until after 1873. While the Army imported craftsmen and clerical staff from the North in the Fall of 1863 and hired primarily contrabands (escaped enslaved people) as laborers, Baucom's skills, knowledge of the area, and enterprising mindset would have been useful to the Union, particularly in construction of numerous supply warehouses and buildings to house their administrative offices. By early 1864, Nashville's population had grown to an estimated 50,000, with 18,000 being nonmilitary employees of the Federal Army. Although Baucom's name is not on the available Union lists of civilian employees, he supported his family somehow, most likely by working for the Army. Possibly he was already acquainted with W. R. Cornelius who became the "Government Undertaker" and worked with him in the related trade of recording deaths, shipping bodies to hometowns, and marking burial sites with wooden markers.[23]

Though relatively safe within Union lines, life—and death—continued for the Baucoms. On September 20, 1864, Baucom purchased a lot in Nashville City Cemetery, and baby Mary Virginia who died the previous day, just four hours old, was buried there. His sister Susan and her husband, William Peach, were also living in Nashville during the war. Peach, too, owned a lot in City Cemetery where his wife was buried after her death on March 14, 1865. Her deteriorated plain marble tablet appears to have the slanted "wife of," "born," and "Died" characteristics of Baucom's carving, but no decorative elements. Shortly after war's end, C. Baucom & Co., General Agents advertised in the July 1865 *Nashville Daily Union* newspaper:

> **Intelligence Office.**
> All persons wanting Mechanics, Clerks, House servants, Wood-Choppers, Cooks—men or women—white or colored, would do well to call at our office, No. 60½ North Cherry street [*sic*], and register their wants. Persons desiring situations will do the same. See sign at the Door.[24]

To have been able to promote an employment agency so soon after war's end indicates not only Baucom's entrepreneurial initiative, but also financial reserves and a circle of potential employees as well as clients. And to have made connections with various laborers and tradesmen during the war indicates he may have been employed by the Union to perform something like general contracting work because ordinary civilians would have been unlikely to have interacted with such workers. Baucom's name was listed in the July 10, 1866, Nashville newspaper as having "appeared on the Poll Books of '64 and '65," and thus he was among the persons "Who Have a Right to Vote Under the New Law"—evidence that he was in good standing with the federal government. The 1865, 1866, and 1867 Nashville City Directories showed Baucom living at 48 S. Cherry and in the latter two years with an "intelligence office" at 60 ½ N. Cherry, but there is no mention of stonework. In October 1866, a cholera epidemic was raging in Middle Tennessee, and one newspaper noted that "Mr. C. Baucom, who resides in Nashville, but was taken sick at Shelbyville while on business, is recovering." Exactly what type of business was not stated. If he continued stone carving, no physical location is in records reviewed to date. Only five markers dated between 1861 and 1866 are attributed to him. Battling cholera may have weakened his body as he died slightly more than a year later on November 22, 1867, from typhoid pneumonia and was buried in Nashville City Cemetery.[25]

Even though the Civil War did not directly kill Baucom, privations of war certainly led to the demise of his stone carving career as his customer base was financially destitute. In addition, by the time of his death, the forty-eight-year-old Baucom may have physically lacked the strength needed to carve stone daily, though he could have had profitable years ahead as an employment agency owner during postwar rebuilding. Nevertheless, his stone carving career of approximately three decades left at least nineteen weeping willows on obelisks, fourteen cemetery mourner motif markers, sixteen with other decoration, and 115 unadorned gravestones standing as testament to his skill and artistry in graveyards across southern Middle Tennessee at a time when most local carvers lacked the inspiration and talent to execute such artistic designs. Because he signed a few distinctive stones, Baucom's legacy can now be venerated.[26]

Nancy Adgent's study of Augustus Saint Gaudens' funerary art was published in *Markers* 34 and she has written several articles for the *AGS Quarterly*, as well as other publications including ABC-Clio's *Women in the American Civil War Encyclopedia*, *Tennessee Encyclopedia of*

History & Culture, and *The Tennessee Conservationist*. She wrote the text for *Deep East Texas Grave Markers: Types, Styles, and Motifs* with photographs and editing by fellow AGS members, Perky Beisel and George Avery. Four cemeteries she co-nominated were placed on the National Register of Historic Places. After a twenty-five-year career as a commercial property/casualty insurance underwriter and supervisor, Nancy earned a master's in history/public history from Middle Tennessee State University. Now retired from the Rockefeller Archive Center in New York, she is based near Nashville and continues to research and write, focusing on gravestones. She is serving a second time as AGS Archives Committee Chair.

Acknowledgments

The author thanks Dr. Carroll Van West for including me in a proposed project at Mars Hill Cemetery which led me to discover a Baucom signed stone, launching my research. Also, thanks to Karin Sprague and Laurel Gabel for their expert assistance regarding lettering and to Judi Trainor for supplying photographs of cemetery mourner gravestones in Massachusetts.

Notes

1. John W. Kiser, "A History of the Mars Hill Church and Cemetery," TS (photocopy in author's possession); Nancy G. Marr to Mars Hill Church, Deed Book V, 434–35, Giles County Archives, Pulaski, Tennessee.
2. The signed stones are Beechwood Cemetery, Cornersville: James H. Collins (c. 1833), Floridene Hurt (1846), Martha Jane Hunt Nance (1858); Brick Church Cemetery, Giles County: Unknown (no date—broken stone), Evander Gordon (1833); First Presbyterian Church Cemetery, Fayetteville: James Russell (1842); Old Graveyard Memorial Park, Pulaski: Sarah H. Potter (1849), Aurelia T. Batte (1853); Maplewood Cemetery, Pulaski: Harriet Perkins (1850), Dr. Peter W. Martin (1854), Emily Jane Martin (1854), Judeth M. Burch (1855), Thomas Knight (1855); Mt. Ararat Cemetery, Lawrenceburg: E. E. Meek (1848), Mary M. Meek (1849), Dr. Josiah F. Atkins (1857); City Cemetery, Lawrenceburg: Ferd F. Bentley (1856); Ewing Family Graveyard Lewisburg: Ewing children (1845); New Hope Cemetery, Cornersville: illegible name (1840); Old Mars Hill Cemetery, Marshall County: Samuel Kincaid (1857).
3. For example, carvers Hiram and Will Presnell Remine are mentioned in "Washington College Academy Historic District" nomination form for the

National Register of Historic Places, Tennessee Historical Commission, 2002, National Park Service, https://npgallery.nps.gov/NRHP/GetAsset/a10c0185-8c68-466e-b2be-86a7f532f536. "Maplewood Cemetery" nomination form for the National Register of Historic Places, Tennessee Historical Commission, 2005, National Park Service, https://npgallery.nps.gov/GetAsset/a2ef5961-c201-4dbd-ab73-4c3151dfde6c/. Nashvillian William Edmondson, a self-taught African American carver who began his career in the 1930s, is the subject of Edmund L. Fuller, *Visions in Stone* (University of Pittsburgh Press, 1973). Richard Finch studied the unusual "comb" grave marker style found on the Cumberland Plateau near Crossville, Tennessee, however, he did not identify any makers, Richard C. Finch, "The Tennessee Comb Grave Tradition," TS, e-mail attachment to author, January 11, 2014. Harriette Merrifield Forbes, *Gravestones of Early New England and the Men Who Made Them, 1653–1800* (Pyne, 1955). See also Ralph Bailey, "William T. White (1823–1870): A Monumental Southern Stonecutter," *Markers* 38 (2022): 92–120; Terry G. Jordan, *Texas Graveyards: A Cultural Legacy* (University of Texas Press, 1982); M. Ruth Little, *Sticks & Stones: Three Centuries of North Carolina Gravemarkers* (University of North Carolina Press, 1998); Daniel W. Patterson, *The True Image: Gravestone Art and the Culture of Scotch Irish Settlers in the Pennsylvania and Carolina Backcountry* (University of North Carolina Press, 2012).

4. Vicky Hilton Cunningham, email message to author with attached Cader Baucom Jr. Bible pages, July 7, 2022; Jim Baucom, "The Ancestors of Susan Fowler, Wife of Cader Baucom," Genealogy.com, https://www.genealogy.com/forum/surnames/topics/baucom/769/; United States Census, 1800, 1810, 1820, 1830, 1840, 1850, 1860, 1870, 1880, Heritage Quest Online via Tennessee Electronic Library, https://tntel.info/resource/heritagequest-online. Siblings were: Wilson (1799–1849) m. Christiana Creek; Elizabeth (1800–1854) m. Bradley Gambill; John (1801–1878) m. Mary Polly Wilson; Willis (1802–1883) m. Elizabeth Wilson; Charlotte (c.1807–>1880) m. Jonas Sutton; Nancy (c. 1810–>1880) m. Rev. Josiah Wilson; Susan (1813–1865) m. William Lewis Peach. (Susan's name is sometimes in records as Susannah, however, because her grave marker has Susan, I use that spelling.) "A Wilson Family History and Genealogy," Weebly.com, http://wilsonfamilygenealogy.weebly.com/josiah-thomas-moses-unknown.html; Banks McLaurin, Jr., editor, *Baucom Families in the United States*, (n.p., 1978), Internet Archive, https://archive.org/details/baucom-families-in-the-us-part-3-20210707-0001/Baucom%20Families%20in%20the%20US%20Part%201_20210707_0001/. Sibling birth and death dates are best guesses based on some differences in the above sources. Photo for Rev. Thomas James Hall, d. 1859, available at findagrave.com, https://www.findagrave.com/memorial/85695681/thomas-james-hall; Marshall County Historical Society, "Churches, Presbyterians," *Marshall County, Tennessee: A Sesquicentennial History* (Walsworth, 1986), 53–58.

5. US Census, 1840. Cader Jr.'s mother is most often referenced in records as Susanna. Susan G. Daniel, comp., *Cemeteries and Graveyards of Rutherford County, Tennessee* (Rutherford County Historical Society, 2005). One of Baucom's brothers and a sister married Wilson siblings, another brother married their aunt, and his mother is buried in one of the Wilson family cemeteries on land previously in Williamson County, but now in Rutherford County. Williamson County, Marriages, FamilySearch, https://www.familysearch.org/en/search/full-text/results?f.collectionId=M9J1-QQT&q.anyPlace=Williamson, Tennessee, United States; US Census, 1850; Lawrence County Marriages, Box 4, File 20, Lawrence County Archives, Leoma, Tennessee; Cader Baucom Jr. Bible.
6. Cynthia Baucom advertised her Pulaski millinery business in *The Western Star,* May 31, 1849, Newspapers.com, Southeast Collection, https://newscomse.newspapers.com/image/586573432/?pqsid=ewJCbH9gQgaHORvvrZHFWQ%3A40159%3A1319922762; US Census, 1850; Rutherford County Daily Court Minute Book A-A, April term 1852, 456, Rutherford County Archives, Murfreesboro, Tennessee.
7. The Sutton's personal property value rose from $2,000 in 1850 to $5,200 in 1860 with real property of $8,000, US Census, 1850, 1860. Cader Baucom Jr.'s Bible has Cynthia's first initial as S for Synthia; I use Cynthia per her tombstone, their marriage license, and other records. "Dress Making, Etc.," *Pulaski Gazette,* September 17, 1852, Newspapers.com, https://newscomse.newspapers.com/search/results/?date=1852&keyword=Baucom. I have not found a marriage record to Mary White; however, they must have married before June 1853 as their son, Thomas M., was born April 8, 1854, per their Bible; US Census, 1850, 1860. Cader Jr.'s children listed in his Bible were: Anney Janthy (1843–1935); Verlinda Angeline (1845–1934) m. Quinn; Sephronia Susannah (1848–c.1865); Cornelia Josephine (1850–1899) m. Tyner; Cynthia Anne (1852–1934); Thomas Martin (1854–?); Ophelia Victoria (1857–1932) m. Dews; John Cader (1859–1886); Mary Virginia (1864–1864).
8. U.S. Census, 1840, 1850; Williamson County, Marriages, Family Search, https://www.familysearch.org/ark:/61903/3:1:3QHV-B35R-2JJF?view=fullText, Image 584, Image Group Number 008960019; "James Peach," Findagrave.com, https://www.findagrave.com/memorial/7804593/james_peach. Peach (1820–1850) "was a stone mason and laid stone on the state capital in Nashville. Named his son after the architect of the capital, William Strickland." This James Peach was the half-brother of William Peach who married Susan Baucom. Bobbye C. Winston, "Peach Family, Pickens County, AL," RootsWeb, https://freepages.rootsweb.com/~kithandkin2000/genealogy/peachfamily.htm.
9. The apprenticeship ended a year later, and Mary was released to Job Coker. She was likely a millinery apprentice for Baucom's wife although she may have been taught to trace lettering or design guidelines on gravestones. Alan N. Miller, *Middle Tennessee's Forgotten Children: Apprentices from 1784 to 1902*

(Genealogical, 2004), 99; Court Minutes, November 4, 1844, Lawrence County, Tennessee, FamilySearch, https://www.familysearch.org/ark:/61903/3:1:3QS7-89P3-4JS?view=explore, image 281, Image Group Number: 007642970.

10. Douglas Keister, *Stories in Stone: A Field Guide to Cemetery Symbolism and Iconography* (Gibbs Smith, 2004), 62–63, 79–80.
11. Maine, New Jersey, and South Carolina comparisons are among the author's photographs, and Plymouth and Harvard, Massachusetts, photographs were provided by Judi Trainor. See other examples on Findagrave.com: https://www.findagrave.com/memorial/43032617/mary-virginia-bowman; https://www.findagrave.com/memorial/48073631/rose-mullin; https://www.findagrave.com/memorial/9306820/hannah-williams#view-photo=63183583.
12. "John Baucom," Findagrave.com, https://www.findagrave.com/memorial/24096858/john-r-baucom. Sale of house and lot "where I reside and have my stone yard and office," deed recorded in October 1858, McLaurin, *Baucom Families*. The signature "C. Baucum & Co., Shelbyville, Tenn," on the 1858 Nance stone is a departure from his usual surname spelling as shown in his Bible and other marker signatures. I suspect it was done by a letter cutter who did not know the usual spelling.
13. James Tibensky, review of *The Search for Henry Cross* by W. Douglas Hartley, *AGS Newsletter* 5, no. 3 (Summer 1981): 6, AGS Archive via Internet Archive, https://archive.org/details/newsletterofasso113asso; Francis Y. Duval and Ivan B. Rigby, "Ohio Memorial Images," *AGS Newsletter* 7, no. 3 (Summer 1983): 5, AGS Archive via Internet Archive, https://archive.org/details/newsletterofasso113asso; Little, *Sticks & Stones*, 228.
14. Cynthia Baucom, Findagrave.com, https://www.findagrave.com/memorial/7360912/cynthia_anna_elizabeth_baucom; Cader Baucom Jr. Bible.
15. *The Marble-Workers' Manual*, trans. M. L. Booth (New York City, 1856), 255–56, Internet Archive, https://archive.org/details/marbleworkersman00unse. US Census, 1850, Giles County, Tennessee.
16. US Census 1850; US Census 1850—Slave Schedules, Heritage Quest via Tennessee Electronic Library (accessed DATE; the website originally cited in this paper no longer works); McLaurin, *Baucom Families*, cites several deeds for sale and purchase of enslaved people from 1851 through 1857; Seventh Census of the United States, Productions of Industry, June 30, 1850, Giles County, Tennessee, Heritage Quest via Tennessee Electronic Library (Accessed August 27, 2023; some components of the Tennessee Electronic Library are only available to Tennessee residents).
17. "Cader Baucom, Stone Cutter, &c.," *Pulaski Gazette*, October 17, 1851, January 23, 1852, and September 17, 1852; Cader Baucom Jr. Bible; Letter to the editor, *Pulaski Citizen*, June 8, 1866, Newspapers.com, Southeast Collection, https://newscomse.newspapers.com/search/?query=Baucum&t=1666.
18. "Nashville Steam Marble Works," *Nashville Union & American*, January 25, 1854, Newspapers.com, Southeast Collection, https://newscomse.newspapers

.com/image/603883587/?match=1&terms=Sloan&pqsid=iT_t1sNDNdHS0nn5-N6LgA:32274:1080764359.

19. McLaurin, *Baucom Families,* references Giles County Deed Book Z, 239, recorded October 25, 1858; US Census 1860; US Census 1860—Slave Schedules, Heritage Quest via Tennessee Electronic Library (Accessed August 27, 2023; some components of the Tennessee Electronic Library are only available to Tennessee residents).
20. US Census 1850, 1860; "Bedford County," *History of Tennessee* (reprint ed., Southern Historical, 1988), 872.
21. Walter T. Durham, *Reluctant Partners: Nashville and the Union* (Tennessee Historical Society, 1987), xii; John C. Spence, *A Diary of the Civil War* (Rutherford County Historical Society, 1993), 82; Larry H. Whiteaker, "Civil War," in *Tennessee Encyclopedia of History & Culture,* edited by Carroll Van West (Rutledge Hill, 1998), 168–71; James M. McPherson, *Battle Cry of Freedom: The Civil War Era* (Ballentine Books, 1989), 430–31, 600–01; US Department of the Interior, National Park Service, Civil War Soldiers and Sailors Database, https://www.nps.gov/civilwar/soldiers-and-sailors-database.htm.
22. Cader Baucom Jr. Bible; Nancy Adgent Morgan, "Fannie Battle, From Spy to Samaritan: A Private Woman in Public Places" (MA thesis, Middle Tennessee State University, 2003), 12–18; Durham, *Reluctant Partners,* xii–xiv.
23. Durham, *Reluctant Partners,* 298; Reply to Letter to the Editor, *Nashville Daily Union,* October 16, 1864, Newspapers.com, Southeast Collection, https://newscomse.newspapers.com/image/78290171/?match=1&terms=Cornelius&pqsid=dR4Eq9sXtjQVRLYFZV4veQ%3A95857%3A1440331843; Department of Veterans Affairs, National Cemetery Administration, "History of Government-Furnished Headstones and Markers," https://www.cem.va.gov/history/hmhist.asp; Durham, *Reluctant Partners,* 20–21; James Lee McDonough, *Nashville: The Western Confederacy's Final Gamble* (University of Tennessee Press, 2004), 129; National Archives and Records Administration, Civil War Union Noncombatant Personnel, Record Group 92-Records of the Office of the Quartermaster General, "List of Wagonmasters, Teamsters, Laborers, and Other Employees, August 1861–October 1862," https://catalog.archives.gov/id/131043647; *Nashville Daily Union,* October 16, 1864.
24. "Baucom" and "Peach," Nashville City Cemetery Association, Metropolitan Nashville/Davidson County Archives, https://nashville.contentdm.oclc.org/digital/collection/nr/id/2454, and https://nashville.contentdm.oclc.org/digital/collection/nr/id/2942/rec/2; Cader Baucom Jr. Bible; "Susan Peach," Findagrave.com, https://www.findagrave.com/memorial/9048944/susannah-peach; *Nashville Daily Union,* July 27, 1865, Chronicling America: Historic American Newspapers, Library of Congress, https://chroniclingamerica.loc.gov/lccn/sn83025718/1865-07-27/ed-1/seq-4/.
25. "Franchise: Who Have a Right to Vote Under the New Law, The Names as They Appeared on the Poll Books of '64 and '65," *Republican Banner,* July 10, 1866,

Newspapers.com, Southeast Collection, https://newscomse.newspapers.com/image/604875244/?pqsid=NPSuW_r2JKhbe_6BomPqgA%3A119650%3A1937470394; "Bancom" [*sic*], Singleton's Nashville Business Directory 1865, Tennessee State Library & Archives online, https://web.archive.org/web/20091022201002/http:/www.tennessee.gov/tsla/ArchiveIt/1865/index1865.html; King's Nashville City Directory 1866, 1867, Tennessee State Library & Archives online, https://wayback.archive-it.org/1771/20100112211815/http://www.tennessee.gov/tsla/ArchiveIt/1867/index1867.html (Accessed January 29, 2023; some components of the Tennessee Electronic Library are only available to Tennessee residents); "Shelbyville: Ravages of the Epidemic," *Republican Banner,* October 4, 1866, Newspapers.com, Southeast Collection, https://newscomse.newspapers.com/image/604876600/?match=1&terms=Shelbyville&pqsid=F6C2iduxDg9t5M8uVQBLZA%3A35428%3A2083477369; "Mortuary: Report on Interments in the City Cemetery during the month of November, 1867," *Nashville Union & Dispatch,* December 3, 1867, Chronicling America: Historic American Newspapers, Library of Congress, https://chroniclingamerica.loc.gov/lccn/sn85038521/1867-12-03/ed-1/seq-3/.

26. This count is as of May 1, 2025, and includes only stones I have photographed. Several more recorded on the Find a Grave website appear to be Baucom's work. Each inscribed pedestal is counted; however, only the signed and/or decorated one is counted as a signed and/or decorated marker.

Frontispiece. Pauper's Section left half of photo, Thornrose Cemetery, Staunton, November 2, 2024. Photograph by the author.

Dying Impoverished

The Funerary Rites, Gravestones, and Cemeteries of the Poor

Lynn Rainville

HISTORICAL CONTEXT OF POOR RELIEF

A once widespread American social assistance program has its surprising roots in the forty-third year of the reign of Queen Elizabeth I. That year, 1601, the "Acte for the Reliefe of the Poore" was passed and served as the foundation for centuries of care for and supervision of impoverished citizens. In Britain, church parishes were the administrative units responsible for poor relief, but the system evolved to include almshouses and workhouses (for paupers who were able-bodied). It even included apprenticeships for poor children.[1]

The British colonies in America replicated many aspects of this system, including the role of church wardens, sending children to apprentice with tradesmen, and, in 1642, passing a set of laws "for the relief of the diverse poore people that [are] . . . disabled to labor by reason of sickness, lameness or age."[2] After a century of church-led efforts, the House of Burgesses approved plans to establish separate "poorhouses" and "workhouses" in two Virginian communities: Nansemond (1742) and Williamsburg (1755).[3] For the rest of the eighteenth century, care for the poor occurred at two municipal levels: "outdoor relief," whereby churches and counties gave cash and clothing to indigent residents living with family or neighbors, and "indoor relief," where cities and counties built poor farms to house paupers. After the American Revolution and separation from the Anglican Church, the Virginia General Assembly gave localities control of pauper aid and established the locally elected position of "Overseer of the Poor" or "Superintendent."[4] The overseers took over the supervision of the poorhouses and workhouses built by the vestries and built new institutions when needed. Over the next several generations, the General Assembly modified the legislation to clarify who should receive aid, for example, they excluded "vagrants." The publicly elected and supported overseer of the poor continued to "provide for the poor, lame, blind and other inhabitants of the district, not able to maintain themselves."[5] The overseers, in turn, were usually the ones responsible for hosting funerary rites and burying the dead.

By the start of the twentieth century, most independent cities and counties in Virginia had established poorhouses to care for their paupers (Figures 1 and 2). These institutions remained popular until the passage of the Social Security Act in 1935, when other resources were deployed for impoverished citizens. As early as 1926, the State Board of Public Welfare issued a report titled *The Disappearance of the County Almshouse in Virginia*. In it, the author argued for a system of "district homes" to replace the poorhouses. That same year, thirty-three of Virginia's county farms closed their doors.[6] Despite these recommendations, dozens of Virginian poor farms remained open until the last quarter of the twentieth century.[7] Between the late nineteenth and mid- to late twentieth century, the state financed other institutions that included impoverished residents: asylums, prisons, and orphanages. Each of these institutions also managed the burial of their residents; those sites will be discussed later in this article. This article uses the burial sites of paupers in the Commonwealth of Virginia as case studies with national implications for the historic mortuary care afforded to impoverished residents.

POORHOUSE RESIDENTS

To give a sense of the reach and scale of poor farms, in 1850, Virginian municipalities were caring for 5,118 paupers (out of a total Virginian population 1,421,661) and in 1860, that number had risen by seventeen percent to 6,027 (at the same time the state's population had risen to 1,596,318).[8] Most of these institutions separated the impoverished residents by sex, in order to avoid adding future paupers, and segregated residents by race if they had space in the domestic quarters, a separation that did not always persist in death. While it may seem unnecessary to describe who the inmates of poor farms were, it was not simply impoverished Virginians.

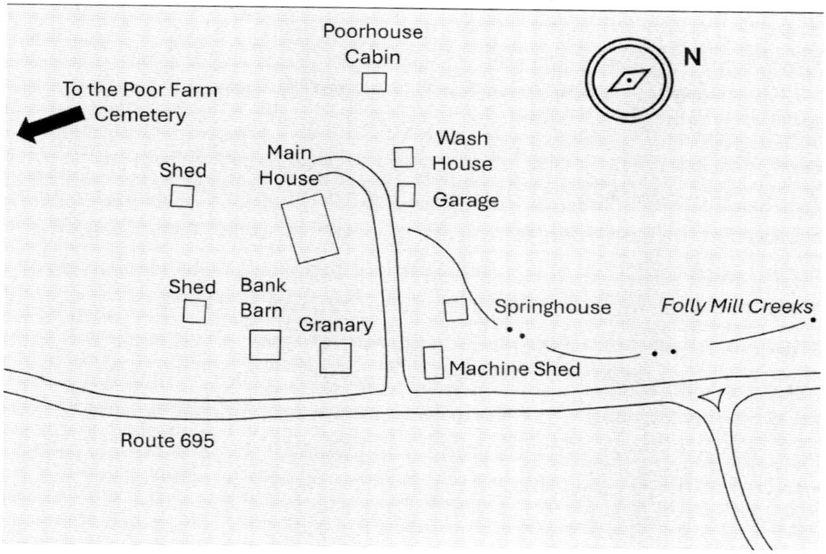

Figure 1. Layout for a typical Virginian poorhouse, Arbor Hill, Augusta County. The overseer and his family lived in the "main house." The cemetery is southwest of the residences. Redrawn from Ellen Finamore's submission for the "Augusta County Poor House" to the Virginia Historic Landmarks Commission, Survey Form (1980, page 2). Unpublished typescript, Augusta County Historical Society.

Figure 2. Shenandoah County Almshouse. Mackenzie Grimes Collection, Truban Archives, Shenandoah County Library, Edinburg, Virginia.

Most indigent Virginians struggled throughout this period without any local or state support. Residents of the poorhouses were sent there by relatives and/or local officials. These community members applied their moral judgements to differentiate between "worthy" and "unworthy poor." By their standards, the former included (white) children and widows, physically infirm, mentally ill, and some elderly folks, whereas the latter were described as lazy, misfits, tramps (later "hobos"), or criminals.[9] Individuals identified by municipal authorities as worthy of care received local support through three main venues: (1) at the homes of their neighbors (who were paid a stipend for this care), (2) churches (Anglican, and later, other denominations), and (3) poor farms or, within urban areas, almshouses.[10] The burial location of a pauper varied, in part, depending on where they received their care.

PAUPER BURIALS AND MORTUARY PRACTICES

Some of the earliest pauper care in the American colonies was "outdoor relief," where relatives or neighbors were given a stipend for taking care of the impoverished. These payments included reimbursements for terminal healthcare and funerals. For example, in 1782, Sarah Turner, of Staunton, "humbly begg[ed]" the overseers "that your Worships will . . . allow me What your Worships think proper" for the care of her neighbor, the dying Sarah Price. "[H]er disorder was such as is not prudent for a Woman to Mention and her smell was such as no person could bear the Room," said Turner. After caring for Ms. Price for two weeks, Sarah washed her corpse, dug her grave, and "attended her till buried."[11] And while this archival entry doesn't specify where Sarah was buried, it was most likely the pauper section within the local Episcopal Churchyard. Over a century later, some municipalities still preferred financing this "outdoor" relief instead of building poorhouses. For example, the city of Alexandria found it "more economical to pay for the care of its poor, than to maintain the poor-house" and continued, as of 1903, to pay local residents to care for paupers. If hospital care was needed, they transferred the individual to a nearby infirmary at a cost of $15 a month.[12] The paupers who died while "boarded out" were probably buried in the "potter's section" of public cemeteries.[13]

Paupers who died while living at a rural "poorhouse" or urban "almshouse" usually received a standard series of procedures that ranged from doctor's visits to graveside ceremonies. The overseer of the poor was responsible for administering this care. They, in turn, often paid professionals to assist in this palliative and postmortem care. For example, in 1830, Washington County paid Sarah Wallis $3.00 "for her services as midwife who delivered Rhoda Crabtree a poor person who died of a child and for nursing her."[14] After a pauper died, the next step was to acquire burial shrouds and build coffins. Sometimes they were made in-house, as with the Patrick County farm where a local resident recounted, "there was a building on the grounds for making coffins which were crude wooden boxes. When one died, they would shroud them, wrap them in a sheet, and place them in one of the handmade coffins."[15] At other farms, local furniture makers or handymen were employed. At the Amherst Poor Farm, a handful of local men were called upon repeatedly to build coffins and dig graves. Between 1846–1849, nine different men built seventeen coffins. Only one of these individuals appears to be a professional craftsman, a carpenter named Curtis Gill (1813–1882).[16] Once the shroud and coffin were ready, either the superintendent, an inmate, or a handyman was paid to dig the grave. In 1873, Charlottesville resident James Kelly was paid $1.50 for "digging a grave for Robb J, Wood" and, later, Adam Whips was paid seventy-five cents for "hauling the corps [*sic*] to the grave."[17]

These costs were itemized by the institution and funded by city coffers, although sometimes they sold the belongings of the deceased to offset the expenses. Local officials carefully tracked these burial expenses, as indicated in an 1849 report from the Rockingham County Overseers of the Poor Farm which specified that "in future the prices which will be allowed by the board for coffins furnished for the burial of paupers shall be fixed as follows to wit for grown persons $3.00 for medium sized coffins $2.00 for children $1.50."[18] After a century of paying for various and sundry mortuary expenses, it's clear why municipalities would want to limit their expenditures to local citizens: John Pluncket's 1803 death in Augusta County cost over eight dollars; the itemized expenses included a coffin, $3.00; shirt, $1.00; overalls and stockings, $1.00; "a Sheet to lay him in," five shillings; a gallon of whiskey, three shillings, six pence; and hauling the corpse to a freshly dug grave, $3.00.[19] Mr. Pluncket's mortuary expenses reveal that superintendents sometimes paid for graveside services, such as ringing a bell, saying a few words, or providing liquid refreshments. These practices date back to the colonial era, including an Augusta County parish that provided two gallons of liquor at a child's eighteenth-century graveside service.[20] Virginian records document a series of institutionally sponsored mortuary rituals, from death to grave. Such acts of benevolence offered the poor a dignity in death that they may not have had in life. But by the late nineteenth century, municipal officials were looking for ways to minimize these expenses. For example, in 1884 the Board of Supervisors in Buckingham County passed a resolution specifying that only "approved and endorsed" burial expenses would be covered.[21] Twentieth-century burials were much plainer, without attendant rituals, ceremonies, or refreshments.

Burial Locations

An impoverished person could be buried in a variety of places, usually based on expediency and cost. I will focus on two of the most distinctive patterns: (1) burial in a "potter's section" within a public burial ground, and (2) burial in a "pauper's cemetery," a separate graveyard associated with a poorhouse.

Potter's Fields

After the irregular layout of colonial-era graveyards, most public burial grounds in nineteenth-century America were laid out in rectangular plots that were sold to individuals for their family's use.[22] This practice created rows of gravestones, even if the distribution of stones within a family plot was more erratic due to unfilled spaces or missing markers. Potter's "fields" are usually identifiable by even more regular lines of stones due to burials in chronological order, rather than kinship ties. These burials are grouped together at the edges or less scenic areas of a cemetery, indicated by small, plain markers with limited inscriptions or symbols.

In 1851, the Thornrose Cemetery Corporation opened the first public cemetery in Staunton. They set aside a potter's field that filled with hundreds of paupers.[23] This section is identifiable by the absence of any stones within an otherwise crowded mortuary landscape (Figure 3). In

Figure 3. Pauper's Section, left half of photo, Thornrose Cemetery, Staunton, November 2, 2024. Photograph by the author.

nearby Charlottesville, the Oakwood Cemetery also contains a section for individuals who died indigent, starting with "Sophie Sheperd's child" in 1883. No stones remain to indicate where this section was.[24] In northern Virginia, the City of Alexandria established a potter's field within the Penny Hill Cemetery, which was used as the municipal burying ground between 1796 and 1976. In 1885, Lewis Dudley (circa 1806–1890), a former gravedigger born enslaved in Prince William County, described burying residents from the poorhouse at this cemetery and, later, burying his wife in a grave that he surrounded with clam shells and a fence.[25] A recent geophysical survey suggests that there are over two thousand unmarked burials at this site, including hundreds of paupers.[26]

Pauper Cemeteries (Rural)

The second popular location for burying paupers was at the site of the poorhouse. In a state-mandated summary of three decades of poor relief in Virginia, 1800–1830, the auditor of public accounts documented poor houses in sixty-three counties and three towns, with forty-three counties and one town lacking the institution.[27] For convenience and cost-savings, most of these poorhouses had an associated graveyard. For this article, I studied the graveyards associated with over four dozen Virginian poor farms (Figure 4). Unfortunately, most of these sites have become overgrown and/or forgotten over time, such as the Patrick County burying ground, which is covered with trees that have been cut for timber several times in the past, possibly damaging the below-ground remains.[28] In Prince William County, a 1996 survey identified thirty graves at the poorhouse, but less than half were marked with a headstone or footstone.[29]

Oral history is sometimes the only lead for the locations of these historic sites. Central Virginia historian Nancy Sorrells interviewed Elizabeth Carter, the daughter of the last overseers of the Augusta County Poor House, Emmett S. Engleman and Lena Harris Engleman. Carter recalled, "When any of the inmates died, my father made them shaped coffins. There is a cemetery in one of the fields southwest of the house at the very edge of the property. My father had it wired off and made nice wooden markers for them."[30] These reminiscences are critical for documenting long-decayed gravemarkers.

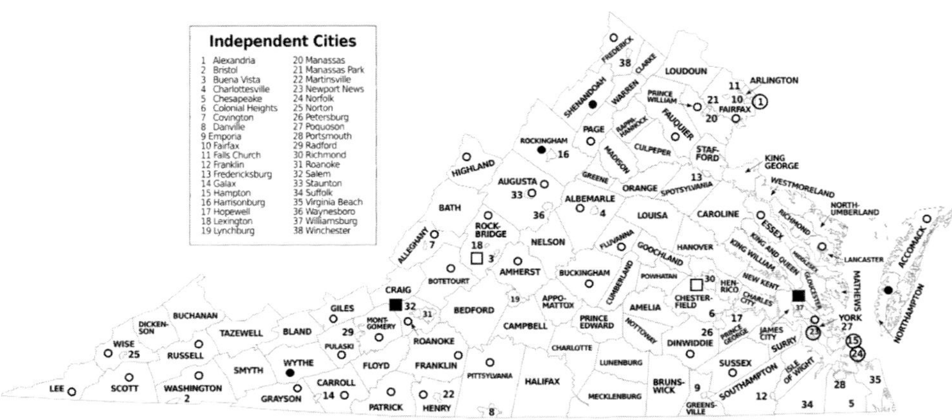

Figure 4. Location of cemeteries analyzed for this article. Circles indicate graveyards with unmarked depressions or uninscribed fieldstones; black dots indicate the presence of inscribed gravestones that contain biographic information. Squares represent burial grounds at prisons, asylums, and orphanages; black squares indicate cemeteries with inscribed markers. The locations are approximate. Map produced by the author.

Pauper Cemeteries (Urban)

The urban manifestation of poor relief was usually referred to as an "almshouse." Just as rural and urban cemeteries often differ in design, pauper cemeteries in cities differed from their rural counterparts in scale (including mass graves on occasion) and were more likely to be damaged by construction or highways. But the overall patterns remain the same, predominantly unmarked depressions or low-cost and plain markers. Prior to World War I, there were only a few large-scale cities in Virginia. In 1900, the largest populations were concentrated in Richmond (85,050), Norfolk (46,624), Petersburg (21,810), Roanoke (21,495), and Newport News (19,635).[31] Each of these cities had an almshouse, but their graveyards appear to be damaged by urban expansion. For example, in Richmond, the city's first almshouse, built before 1810, was surrounded on the south and east by a public, yet segregated, cemetery (Shockoe Hill), a Jewish cemetery, and an African American burial ground. Decades later, city maps elided the last two sites, labelling this area as a "Potter's Field" (Figure 5). Today, this site is mostly buried by an interstate highway, and efforts are ongoing to preserve what remains and highlight the lives of the individuals buried here.[32] Similar destruction occurred at the Roanoke Almshouse or "City Farm." In the mid-twentieth century, the bodies from the pauper graveyard were exhumed to make way for the Roanoke Technical Institute, now Virginia Western Community College, and an interstate exchange. The paupers were reburied at Coyner Springs, located about a dozen miles away.[33] Of the 1,500 reburials, only twenty-seven graves are marked with separate, yet uninscribed, stones. More recently, a city council member is working to erect a memorial to list the names of the former inmates and to create an online portal to provide additional biographic details about each decedent (Figure 6).[34]

Pauper Burials at Other Institutions

Paupers were not just sent to the poorhouse. They were also found in prisons, asylums, and orphanages and, accordingly, buried in those institutional graveyards. Prisons managed their share of natural and state-mandated deaths.[35] In the eighteenth and nineteenth centuries, some urban prisons included burial grounds, such as the Virginia State Penitentiary (in Richmond), which used a spot just outside of the prison

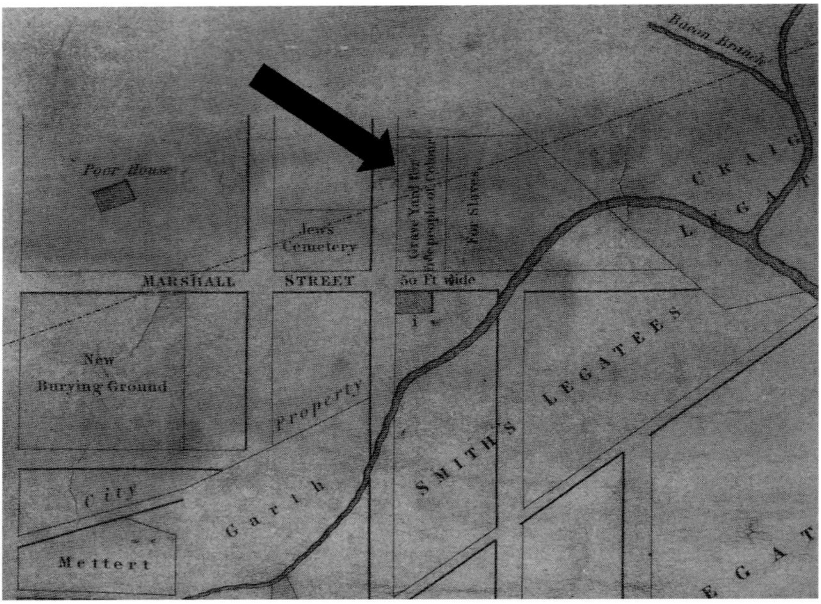

Figure 5a. City of Richmond Almshouse, 1835. Micajah Bates, plan of the City of Richmond. Identifier G3884.R5 1835.B37. "Virginia Memory" at the Library of Virginia, https://rosetta.virginiamemory.com/delivery/DeliveryManagerServlet?dps_pid=IE3527053.

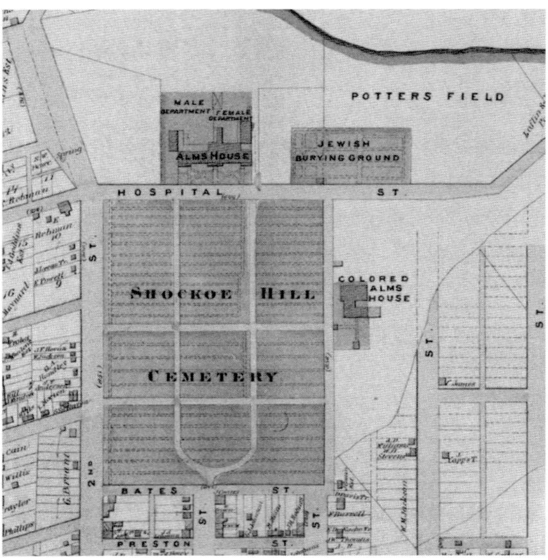

Figure 5b. City of Richmond Almshouses. F. W. Beers, Illustrated atlas of the City of Richmond, 1876. Call Number G1294.R5 B4 1877. Library of Congress Geography and Map Division Washington, D.C., record found via Ancestry.com. Map reveals cartographical erasure of the historic African American cemetery, with the "Potters Field" and "Jewish Burying Ground" listed in their place.

Figure 6. Contemporary marker for the paupers exhumed from the Roanoke City Almshouse and reburied here, Coyner Springs Cemetery, Botetourt County. Photograph by the author.

walls to expediently bury prisoners who died during their incarceration. During the demolition of the two-centuries-old prison, in 1992, the remains of several dozen individuals were uncovered here, many buried in pine boxes.[36] In both urban and rural instances, prisoners sentenced to hang may have been buried at or near the site of the gallows. For example, at Brushy Hills (Rockbridge County), an enslaved man only identified as "Ben" was hanged on November 29, 1850. This court-sanctioned execution was documented in the local newspaper; after his death, "his body was taken down and consigned to the grave prepared at the foot of the gallows."[37] It is not clear if this was a deliberately unmarked grave. Forty years later, a Rockbridge County journalist suggested that the "bodies [from hangings] always became subjects for the dissecting knife instead of being allowed to rest in their graves," a tragic fate that also befell some paupers.[38]

Asylums also included impoverished patients. Earlier, Virginia tried to separate the care of paupers and insane residents by founding the first hospital devoted to treating the mentally ill, incorporated in 1768 as the "Public Hospital for Persons of Insane and Disordered Minds." Later known as Eastern State Hospital, thousands of patients received treatment here and it continues today at a new site. The hospital's cemetery is adjacent to the eighteenth-century location and contains at least 1,200 burials.[39] As with some of the pauper cemeteries, most graves are unmarked, but there are a few dozen inscribed stones, perhaps belonging to individuals whose families contributed to more personalized markers (Figures 7 and 8). Figure 9 illustrates numbered (but not named) gravemarkers that were discarded at the edge of the cemetery, whereas Figure 10 shows one of the numbered markers in situ. A commemorative marker was added in 1986, inscribed with:

> We erect this monument in memory of those persons whom we have known, loved and served through the years. While living they knew the suffering of inner pain, confusion and despair. Now they are at peace in the hands of God where no torment will ever touch them again.

This marker includes the names of former patients, most of whom are presumably buried here.[40]

A third publicly funded institution that overlaps in form and function with poorhouses is the orphanage; they were popular in the 1800s and peaked in numbers around the 1930s. In Salem, the Baptist Church founded an orphanage in 1892, caring for children whose parents were impoverished or dead. The associated cemetery, the Baptist Orphanage Cemetery, does not contain any gravestones. A marker placed there in 2007 commemorates seven children who died between 1893 and 1934 and, presumably, there are many more unmarked graves.[41]

Pauper Gravestones and Commemorative Markers

My analysis of pauper gravestones in this article is based on two sets of data: (1) a study of over three dozen poor farm and almshouse cemeteries in Virginia that are documented, to varying degrees, in the Find a Grave

Figure 7. Inscribed stones, Eastern State Hospital, Williamsburg, December 26, 2023. Photograph by the author.

Figure 8. George McClellan, 1929, Eastern State Hospital, Williamsburg, December 26, 2023. Photograph by the author.

Figure 9. Discarded, Eastern State Hospital, Williamsburg, December 26, 2023. Photograph by the author.

Figure 10. In situ. Eastern State Hospital, Williamsburg, December 26, 2023. Photograph by the author.

database and, (2) on-site visits that I have made to an additional dozen pauper cemeteries in central Virginia (see Figure 4). By supplementing these burial sites with death records, I reviewed over 1,500 pauper deaths at over fifty different poor farms. Only a few dozen of these individuals were buried under gravemarkers inscribed with their names. Most of these paupers lie in unmarked depressions. Of the fifty-five cemeteries studied for this article, 70 percent lacked any form of above-grave marker. These cemeteries are overgrown fields and/or areas with construction disturbance.

Sixteen of the cemeteries have a combination of marked and unmarked graves. The deathscape at the Fauquier County Poorhouse follows this pattern: seventy people buried in a mix of uninscribed stones and unmarked depressions.[42] As with other strategically underprivileged groups, such as enslaved individuals, these gravestones were made from locally available materials, such as fieldstones or small boulders. These stones were rarely inscribed with the names of the deceased. However, some poor farms numbered each stone, which, presumably, corresponded to a written list of names. Unfortunately, these lists rarely survive. Instead, we see situations like the Almshouse in Chatham, with over sixty visible gravesites, twenty marked with uninscribed stones and forty-one adorned with small brass markers. Those markers are numbered, but one stone contains the number 188, suggesting that at least 147 stones (or their brass markers) have gone missing. Moreover, the list that connects the numbers to names has not been found.[43]

Only six of the sites reviewed in this article included gravestones inscribed with the names of the deceased: Northampton County (one stone), Rockingham County (three stones, one of which is a footstone), Salem (one stone for multiple people), Shenandoah County (sixteen stones), Williamsburg (several dozen stones), Wythe County (two stones). These inscribed stones are store-bought marble and granite, but are limited to nearly two-dimensional, short headstones and horizontal, granite memorials, flush with the ground. Most inscriptions are just the deceased's name and dates of birth/death. In a few cases there is an additional adage such as "At Rest" (Virdie Fitzwater, Rockingham County) or reference to a kinship connection, such as "sons of" (unnamed infant twins at Shenandoah).

The Pleasant Valley Almshouse Cemetery (Rockingham County) contains over four-hundred graves, but just two are inscribed, Peter Wimer

(1830–1908, includes his footstone) and Virdie Fitzwater (1909–1912) (Figures 11 and 12). It is unclear why these two individuals were singled out for commemoration; perhaps their families contributed the money for the marble memorials. Similarly, family or community members may have contributed money to erect inscribed gravestones for two Confederate soldiers who died at the Wytheville (Wythe County) poor farm (Figures 13 and 14). Hugh Warf's first wife predeceased him and was buried in a different state, over five hundred miles away, a reminder that paupers are often buried in isolation from their family members.[44] Venable's stone was probably erected decades ago, while Warf's stone may have been sponsored by a modern-day group, given its style and lack of weathering. There are at least two dozen additional paupers buried at this cemetery in unmarked graves. In 2001, the community erected a granite memorial inscribed "for the no longer invisible people."[45]

The Shenandoah County Poor Farm contained the most uniformly inscribed gravestones, but it is clear that the earliest deaths, in the nineteenth century, lie under unmarked graves. With one exception, only the individuals who died since 1989 received inscribed stones (Figure 15). Maybe the addition of the cemetery to the National Register of Historic Places in 1993 was a catalyst for marking the more recent graves.[46] Perhaps the most aptly inscribed gravestone is found in Machipongo (Northampton County) where George E. Scott's (1788–1881) epitaph reads, "Blessed are you who are poor for yours is the kingdom of God . . . Luke 6:20." The 1880 Federal Census for "Defectives, Dependent, and Delinquent Class" listed Mr. Scott as "crippled."[47] He appeared in multiple Northampton Census records, including 1870 when he was living with a widow, Emily Fitchett, and working as a laborer.[48] It is not clear why or when he was "sent to the poorhouse."

Due to the limited examples in my dataset, I was unable to determine whether the morphology of pauper graves parallels changing designs in other American gravestones. While other Virginian gravestones show distinct morphological and symbolic changes between the 1700s and the present, such as the transition from winged deaths heads carved in slate to shaking hands carved in marble, the pauper stones are almost always quite plain. A more comprehensive study of pauper graves across the country may reveal more robust diachronic patterns.[49]

Figure 11. Peter Wimer, 1908, Pleasant Valley Almshouse Cemetery, Rockingham County, February 3, 2013. Photograph by the author.

Figure 12. Virdie Fitzwater, 1912, Pleasant Valley Almshouse Cemetery, Rockingham County, February 3, 2013. Photograph by the author.

Figure 13. Jesse Venable, 1915, Wytheville, Wythe County, June 24, 2013. Photograph by Martha F. Byrum, https://www.findagrave.com/memorial/112805749/jesse-venable.

Figure 14. Hugh Warf, 1925, Wytheville, Wythe County, June 24, 2013. Photograph by Martha F. Byrum, https://www.findagrave.com/memorial/112815639/hugh-warf.

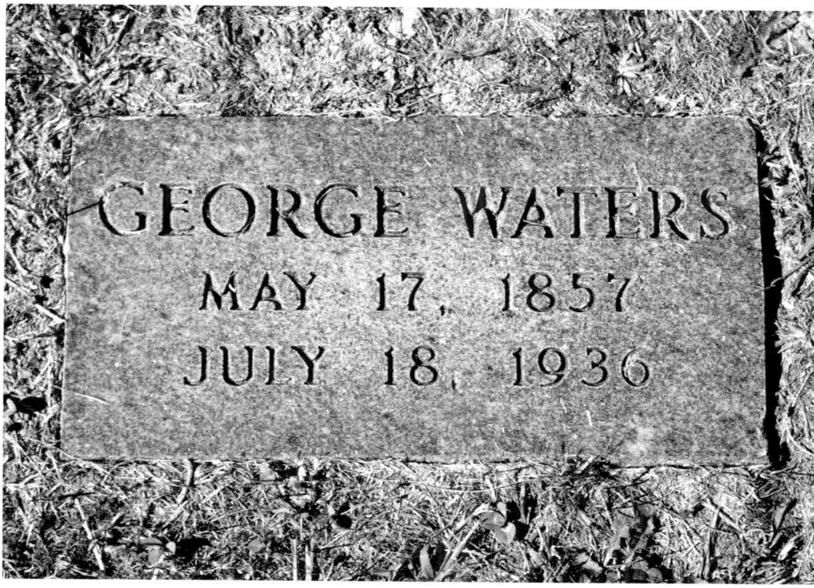

Figure 15. George Waters, 1936, Shenandoah County Poor Farm Cemetery. The post-1980s markers share similar morphologies, February 23, 2020. Photograph by Susan McKnight, https://www.findagrave.com/memorial/29612511/george-waters.

Similarly, because of the small percentage of inscribed stones, it is very difficult to assess whether the burials were organized within the pauper cemeteries by sex, race, ethnicity, or even age. We don't know if overseers of the poor segregated burials by race or made any effort to reserve adjacent spaces for family members, such as mothers and children. Our narrow window into these patterns comes from the handful of inscribed pauper markers and removal reports which contain forensic information about the deceased. In the Newport News Almshouse, the cemetery included Black and white residents buried together in "plain pine boxes."[50] Unfortunately, most archaeological studies of poor farm burial grounds occur because of impending construction, resulting in the exhumation and removal of the bodies, such as the disinterment of human remains from the Alexandria County Almshouse Cemetery in 1939, which were reburied in the potter's field at Penny Hill Cemetery.[51]

Over the past two decades, the once forgotten institution of poorhouses and almshouses has seen a resurgence of interest. Accordingly, some communities have worked to relocate, clean, and commemorate

Figure 16. Virginia Historic Marker, erected in 2001. Photograph by the author.

the last resting places of the former residents. These contemporary memorials take a wide range of forms. In Machipongo (Northampton County), a local craftsman erected a tall white cross at the edge of a woods where paupers were buried.[52] Other municipalities turned to state recognition and memorials, such as Wythe County, which erected a Virginia Highway Marker for the poorhouse in 2001 (Figure 16). The cemetery received a separate marker, donated by Grubb Funeral Home and Wytheville Monument Company.[53] The memorial erected by the Carroll County Board of Supervisors at the site of the exhumed burials once located at the county farm summed up the fate of many pauper burials: "known only to God."[54]

PRESERVATION CHALLENGES

Most of the pauper cemeteries discussed in this article have suffered from neglect or outright destruction. The biggest damage to these sites came from grave robbing and urban development. Throughout the nineteenth century, grave robbers or "body snatchers" did a brisk business in selling cadavers to medical schools, which relied on the bodies for anatomic dissection. Some states went further and passed laws to allow medical schools to use the unclaimed remains of paupers or criminals.[55] Gradually, public outcry against stealing bodies for dissection translated into laws that made it possible for people to donate their bodies to science. For many indigent residents, the damage had already been done. An article from 1930 cites the "unscrupulous undertaker holding the contract for the burial of indigent dead [who were] known to have buried coffins empty of remains but weighted to avoid suspicion" and the practice of burying paupers in shallow graves to increase the ease of exhumation by nearby medical colleges.[56]

A second significant impact on the burials within pauper cemeteries is the pressure of urban development, often slated for previously undesirable or undervalued areas, such as the sites of poorhouses and their graveyards. These pressures damaged countless cemeteries in Virginia, such as the Newport News Almshouse Cemetery, disturbed in 1942 when bulldozers destroyed a child's skull and adult skeletons.[57] Even more recently, in 1997, the burials from the Norfolk Almshouse (founded in 1854, closed in 1929) were unearthed to make room for the construction of a multimillion-dollar addition to the Chesapeake Jail. In this case, the bones were cremated and buried in the nearby Chesapeake Memorial Gardens.[58]

LOCATING PAUPER BURIALS IN YOUR COMMUNITY

The best way to avoid this type of damage is to proactively identify these burial grounds and add them to local and state deeds, tax maps, and planning documents. The first step to locate them is to find your local poor farm(s) or almshouse(s). That task is sometimes as simple as searching a Google map for "Poorhouse Rd.," "Town Farm," or "Paupers Ln." Because poor farms were originally located on less desirable (or at least less expensive) land and were owned by the city/county, the land is often still in use by municipal services, such as trash facilities or SPCAs. In other cases, longtime residents of a locality may remember the location of the poorhouse or even refer to the neighborhood around the site as "the poor farm." Some municipalities have incorporated this terminology into the modern-day use of the site, like Hanover County's "Poor Farm Park."[59]

Occasionally these sites have been added to local, state, or federal historic registers. There are two types of state-sponsored historic markers in the Commonwealth: highway markers and nominations on the state (and sometimes) national historic registry. In Virginia, four communities have nominated their poor farms/almshouses to the Virginia Highway Marker program.[60] A search of the Virginia Landmarks Register, updated in 2023, revealed eight sites (out of over three thousand) that relate to poor farms, almshouses, or "county farms."[61] The register forms, especially ones from more recent nominations, contain useful architectural, archaeological (where relevant), historical, and mortuary data.

A more tedious way to relocate poor farms is to search census records for the residence of the "overseer of the poor." The paupers, often referred to as "inmates" on the federal census, will be listed as part of, or in adjacent, households. This information, combined with deaths recorded in courthouses, can be used to identify individuals who may be buried in poor farm graveyards. A related research task is locating the inmates' death certificates. For example, after the poor farm in Wise[62] (Wise County) was closed in 1954 and two of its buildings were reused for Clinch Valley College (today's University of Virginia at Wise), the location of the cemetery was obscured. However, dedicated researchers have scoured death certificates and posted records for forty-seven individuals whose death certificates listed the "Co. Farm" or "County Home" as the place of death and/or burial.[63] Death certificates were not mandated by the state of Virginia until 1912 (with the formation of the Bureau of Vital Statistics), so this approach is only useful for the past century.[64]

Once you identify former overseers and inmates, descendants may be able to contribute additional information. William Zirk grew up at the Rockingham County Poor Farm where his father and grandfather served as sequential superintendents between 1945–1956. He has spent years collecting information about the 1,200 inmates who once lived there; his research also sheds light on their burials in a nearby cemetery.[65] Moreover, through his and other volunteers' tireless efforts, the community erected a memorial at the cemetery, which includes the names of former residents buried nearby in unmarked graves (Figure 17).

Figure 17. Contemporary memorial, Pleasant Valley Alms Cemetery, February 3, 2013, Rockingham County. Photograph by the author.

If you have identified a burial ground associated with a poor farm/ almshouse and it is not yet recorded with local or state entities, alert your state's historic preservation office and any nearby landowners to ensure that the burials remain undisturbed.[66] As readers of *Markers* are well aware, the information contained within cemeteries and inscribed on gravestones is an invaluable part of American history, and yet, the graves of the American poor are often overlooked. Hopefully more researchers will add information about pauper graves and cemeteries to Find a Grave and other mortuary databases so that we can continue to document and learn from these sites. Rediscovering these sites allows descendants to learn about ancestors who may be missing in family histories and allow researchers to understand the care and distribution of poor relief in America.

After earning her PhD in anthropology and archaeology, **Lynn Rainville** has spent the last twenty-five years as a public historian. She has refined innovative ethnographic, historical, and digital methods while studying Virginia's historic cemeteries, enslaved communities, segregated schools, poor farms, and its role in World War I. Her grant-funded research has produced numerous articles and five books, including *Hidden History: African American Cemeteries in Central Virginia* (University of Virginia Press, 2014) and *Invisible Founders: How Two Centuries of African American Families Transformed a Plantation into a College* (Berghahn Press, 2019). She works as a historic consultant on Virginian history and culture, slavery, and cemeteries.

Notes

1. Walter I. Trattner, *From Poor Law to Welfare State: A History of Social Welfare in America* (Free Press, 1979), 9–10; Brenda Stevenson, *Life in Black and White: Family and Community in the Slave South* (Oxford University Press, 1997), 30.
2. James D. Watkinson, "'Fit Objects of Charity': Community, Race, Faith, and Welfare in Antebellum Lancaster County, Virginia, 1817–1860," *Journal of the Early Republic* 21, no. 1 (Spring 2001): 41–42.
3. These were the approval dates, not the dates of construction. John Patrick Shevock, "Poor Relief in Colonial Virginia" (Master's thesis, University of Virginia, 1979).

4. Initially created in 1780, the Poor Laws and the position of overseer of the poor were expanded in an act from 1819. See *The Revised Code of the Laws of Virginia*, vol. 2 (Thomas Ritchie), Section C 289, "Poor Law," 264–79.
5. *The Revised Code of the Laws of Virginia*, 264–65, 279.
6. Arthur W. James, *Disappearance of the County Almshouse: Back from "Over the Hill"* (Davis Bottom, 1926), 19, 64–71.
7. In 1978, a journalist claimed that the Shenandoah County Almshouse was the last in Virginia, but this claim rests on the imprecise definition and overlapping functions among "almshouses," "poorhouses," and "District Homes." Sue Johnson, "Maurertown Has Only Almshouse Left in Virginia," *Daily News Leader* (Staunton), July 20, 1978, https://www.newspapers.com/image/288192519. But the Waynesboro District Home (housing paupers from the consolidation of nearby poorhouses) remained open until 1999.
8. *The Seventh Census of the United States: 1850, Comparative Table of Population*, US Census Bureau, https://www2.census.gov/library/publications/decennial/1850/1850a/1850a-02.pdf; *Population of the United States in 1860: Virginia*, 518, US Census Bureau, https://www2.census.gov/library/publications/decennial/1860/population/1860a-36.pdf. In both decades, the percentage of Virginians who were classified as "paupers" is miniscule, despite widespread poverty within the state, revealing the highly subjective nature of who was deemed "worthy" of support.
9. Robert W. Kelso, *The History of Public Poor Relief in Massachusetts, 1620–1920* (Houghton Mifflin, 1922), 13, 21–22, 113, 149. One of the first statutes that differentiated the two was the Act of 1536 (in England) which specified that the "worthy poor" were the appropriate object of local relief.
10. Various terms are applied to describe impoverished citizens: paupers, indigents, the poor. And multiple synonyms are used to describe an institution that houses paupers: poor farm (one or two words), poorhouse (one or two words), city or county farm, workhouse, or almshouse (one or two words, mostly used in urban areas).
11. James D. Watkinson, "Rogues, Vagabonds, and Fit Objects: The Treatment of the Poor in Antebellum Virginia," *Virginia Cavalcade* 49, no. 1 (Winter 2000): 20.
12. "Erring and the Poor," *Richmond Times-Dispatch*, February 15, 1903, https://www.newspapers.com/image/827325836.
13. The term "potter's field" is used interchangeably with "pauper's section." The term originated in a biblical passage, Matthew 27:7, which instructs people to bury "strangers" in the place where potters dug for clay, because those spots already contained open trenches.
14. Watkinson, "Rogues," 28.
15. Lucy Clifton Nowlin, quoted in Beverly Belcher Woody, "Residents of the Poorhouse," *Enterprise*, December 14, 2022, https://theenterprise.net/residents-of-the-poorhouse/.

16. "Amherst County (Va.) Overseers of the Poor Minutes, 1844–1870," Circuit Court records (Barcode number 1105839), Library of Virginia; 1850 Federal Census, Amherst County, 110A, residence 545, listed Curtis Gill as a carpenter, Ancestry.com, https://www.ancestry.com/discoveryui-content/view/14817470:8054.
17. Charlottesville records at the Richmond Annex of the Library of Virginia, receipts from May 26, 1873, Albemarle County, Box #3. Courtesy of Alice Cannon.
18. Minutes from the Annual Meeting of the Overseers of the Poor (Rockingham County), June 11, 1849, *Overseers of the Poor Minutes Book I,* "Histories Along the Blue Ridge," https://omeka.lib.jmu.edu/erp/items/show/3828.
19. Watkinson, "Rogues," 28.
20. Joseph A. Waddell, *Annals of Augusta County, Virginia from 1726–1871,* 2nd ed. (C. J. Carrier, 1958), 162.
21. Joanne L. Yeck, *"At a Place Called Buckingham" . . . Historic Sketches of Buckingham County, Virginia,* vol. 2 (Slate River, 2015), 23.
22. These planned landscapes are reform cemeteries, dating to 1796 with the New Burying Ground in New Haven (Connecticut), which were precursors to the Rural Cemetery Movement, which began in the 1830s. Dell Upton, "Gridding the Graveyard," in *Another City: Urban Life and Urban Spaces in the New American Republic* (Yale University Press, 2008), 203–41; Joy Giguere, "'Crowded till They Are Full': Burial Reform in the Early Republic," in *Pleasure Grounds of Death: The Rural Cemetery in Nineteenth-Century America* (University of Michigan Press, 2024), 10–40; Ryan K. Smith, *Death and Rebirth in a Southern City: Richmond's Historic Cemeteries* (Johns Hopkins University Press, 2020), 73.
23. "Town Council," *Valley Virginian,* February 6, 1867, https://www.newspapers.com/image/888587414.
24. "Oakwood Cemetery History_HP," part of the research for the cemetery's historic designation, https://weblink.charlottesville.org/public/0/edoc/793464/Oakwood%20Cemetery%20History_HP.pdf.
25. "Don't Want a Day Fixed," *Alexandria Gazette,* July 21, 1885, https://www.newspapers.com/image/347355430.
26. Nadia E. Johnson and William J. Johnson, *Non-Invasive Geophysical Surveys: Douglass Memorial and Penny Hill Cemeteries, Alexandria, Virginia,* December 2019, 23. Prepared for the City of Alexandria, Virginia, by RHEA Engineers & Consultants, Inc., https://media.alexandriava.gov/docs-archives/historic/info/archaeology/sitereportjohnsongeophysicalsurveysdouglassandpennyhill.pdf.
27. Report of the public auditor, manuscript submitted by James E. Heath, Richmond, December 1830, Library of Virginia, scanned by Robert Vernon 2006. Four of the counties and one town submitted "no report," but presumably they had poorhouses.
28. Woody, "Residents of the Poorhouse."

29. “Poor House,” National Park Service, https://www.nps.gov/prwi/learn/historyculture/poor-house.htm.
30. Nancy Sorrells, “Poor Farm,” author’s personal manuscript files, TS. See Figure 1 for a 1980 map that corroborates the memory of Ms. Carter.
31. Data compiled from the US Federal Census, originally available on the Geospatial and Statistical Data Center of the University of Virginia Library. “Population of Virginia—1900,” http://s1030794421.onlinehome.us/population/pop1900numbers.html.
32. Descendant Lenora McQueen has led efforts to rediscover and preserve the Shockoe Hill African American Burial Ground which lies adjacent to the almshouse cemetery. Ryan K. Smith, “Shockoe Hill African Burying Ground,” Richmond Cemeteries, https://www.richmondcemeteries.org/potters-field/.
33. Ralph Berrier Jr., “The Last Refuge,” *Roanoke Times,* April 19, 2009, https://www.newspapers.com/image/922768535.
34. Randy Walker, “A Quest to Remember Roanoke’s Nameless Dead,” *Cardinal News,* May 6, 2022, https://cardinalnews.org/2022/05/06/a-quest-to-remember-roanokes-nameless-dead/.
35. For a review of state-mandated executions and efforts to halt them see Dale Brumfield, *Closing the Slaughterhouse* (Abolition Press, 2022).
36. Associated Press, “Remains of 46 People Found at Prison, so Far,” *Richmond Times-Dispatch,* March 11, 1992, https://www.newspapers.com/image/831953568.
37. “Execution of ‘Ben,’” *Lexington Gazette,* December 5, 1850. Citation courtesy of Cinder Stanton.
38. “Former Executions in Rockbridge,” *Rockbridge County News,* February 12, 1891, https://www.virginiachronicle.com/?a=d&d=RCN18910212.1.3.
39. Estimate from the names listed in on-site memorials and inscribed gravestones. “Eastern State Hospital Cemetery Memorials,” https://www.findagrave.com/cemetery/50694/eastern-state-hospital-cemetery.
40. On site visit December 23, 2023, data taken from inscribed memorials.
41. Salem Orphanage Cemetery, Findagrave.com, https://www.findagrave.com/memorial/204905585/george-almond-fallwell.
42. Robin Earl, “Fauquier’s Poorhouse History Comes Alive Online—and on Screen,” *Fauquier Times,* April 14, 2022, https://www.fauquier.com/lifestyles/fauquier-s-poorhouse-history-comes-alive-online-and-on-screen/article_bf4f68b4-ba94-11ec-a846-0b930ba768ef.html.
43. “Poorhouse Cemetery—Chatham Memorials,” Findagrave.com, https://www.findagrave.com/cemetery/2427135/poorhouse-cemetery---chatham.
44. Hugh Warf’s wife, Christina Spencer Warf (1836–1911) is buried in the Marvins Cemetery, Brownsville, Tennessee, located over five hundred miles away from her husband. “Christina Spencer Warf,” Findagrave.com, https://www.findagrave.com/memorial/107342316/christina_warf.

45. "Poorhouse Farm Cemetery," Findagrave.com, https://images.findagrave.com/photos/2013/174/CEM2501706_137207265582.jpg.
46. "Shenandoah County Farm," National Register of Historic Places Registration Form, prepared by Shirley Maxwell, James C. Massey, Mary Kell, US Department of the Interior, National Park Service, 1993.
47. 1880 Federal Census Schedules of Defective, Dependent, and Delinquent Classes, Northampton, Enumeration District 82, Schedule page 13, line 8, Ancestry.com, https://www.ancestry.com/discoveryui-content/view/46706:1634.
48. 1870 US Federal Census, Capeville, Northampton, Ancestry.com, https://www.ancestry.com/discoveryui-content/view/37458420:7163.
49. For a sample of inscribed stones from other states, see Livingston County (Illinois), https://genealogytrails.com/ill/livingston/cem_livingston_poor_farm.html; Grayson County (Texas), https://www.findagrave.com/cemetery/2263454/grayson-county-farm-cemetery; Pineville in Wyoming County (West Virginia), https://www.findagrave.com/cemetery/2155406/poor-farm-cemetery; Hillsborough County (New Hampshire), https://www.findagrave.com/cemetery/2431838/poor-farm-cemetery. These examples contain some personally inscribed stones, but also ones adorned with just numbers.
50. "U.S. Housing Project Roadway Tears Through Old Burial Ground," *Daily Press (Newport News)*, August 4, 1942, https://www.newspapers.com/image/230283275.
51. "Old Graveyard is Uncovered in Alexandria," *Loudoun News*, August 3, 1939, https://www.virginiachronicle.com/?a=d&d=LNS19390803.1.6.
52. Connie Morrison, "Project Seeks to Identify and Remember Forgotten Poor," *Delmarva Now*, June 19, 2014, https://www.delmarvanow.com/story/news/local/virginia/2014/06/19/cemetary-mystery/10845177/. The Barrier Islands Center has supported in-depth research into the on-site, former poorhouse and, with Morninglight Films, sponsored a film, *The Almshouse*, a James Spione Film (2024), https://www.pbs.org/video/the-almshouse-cduxjh/.
53. Susan M. Thigpen, "Wythe County Poorhouse Farm," Mountain Laurel, https://mtnlaurel.com/history/791-wythe-county-poorhouse-farm.html.
54. "Poorhouse Farm Cemetery," Findagrave.com, https://www.findagrave.com/cemetery/2501706/poorhouse-farm-cemetery.
55. Edward C. Halperin, "The Poor, the Black, and the Marginalized as the Source of Cadavers in United States Anatomical Education," *Clinical Anatomy* 20 (2007): 490–91; Daina Ramey Berry, *The Price for Their Pound of Flesh* (Beacon Press, 2017), 148–93; Michael Sappol, *A Traffic of Dead Bodies: Anatomy and Embodied Social Identity in Nineteenth-Century America* (Princeton University Press, 2002), 35–36.
56. Allen J. Black, "Robbing Graves in Old Richmond," *Richmond Times-Dispatch*, June 1, 1930, https://www.newspapers.com/image/827822306.
57. "U.S. Housing Project Roadway Tears Through Old Burial Ground."

58. "Where Did the Poor and Infirm Live During the 19th Century? The Norfolk County Poorhouse," *Virginian-Pilot,* August 6, 2019, https://www.pilotonline.com/2018/02/11/where-did-the-poor-and-infirm-live-during-the-19th-century-the-norfolk-county-poorhouse/.
59. "Poor Farm Park," Hanover County, Virginia, https://www.hanovercounty.gov/248/Poor-Farm-Park.
60. Search conducted September 19, 2024, using the search terms: "poor farm," "poorhouse," "almshouse," and "pauper," "Historic Markers," Virginia Department Historic Resources, https://vcris.dhr.virginia.gov/HistoricMarkers/.
61. "Interactive Database of the Virginia Landmarks Register & National Register of Historic Places," Department of Historic Resources, https://www.dhr.virginia.gov/historic-registers/. One site appears in both a highway marker and on the register: Wythe County Poor Farm. Seven distinct sites are recognized in Virginia.
62. The town of "Wise" was originally incorporated as the town of "Gladeville" in 1874; the name was changed in 1924.
63. "James Adams," 1949, certificate 04276–04641, Virginia, US Death Records, 1912–2014, Ancestry.com, https://www.ancestry.com/search/collections/9278/records/2446033.
64. "Virginia Death Certificates, 1912–1987," Familysearch.com, https://www.familysearch.org/search/collection/2377565.
65. Mr. Zirk shares oral histories and remembrances of the Rockingham County Poor Farm in his 2022 talk, "Forgotten People of Rockingham County, in the Poor House," Youtube.com, https://www.youtube.com/watch?v=2oTVs8ZYxo8.
66. For a list of your state's preservation offices, see https://www.nps.gov/subjects/nationalregister/state-historic-preservation-offices.htm.

Frontispiece. Headboard of Henry E. S. Grimston, January 7, 1863. Left image enhanced with black lettering. Public domain.

Restoring Their Honor

Image Forensics Identifies Lost Graves of Union Soldiers

Amy L. Giroux

In order to be able to carry out instructions which I have received directing the re-numbering and marking names on headboards from which original painting is effaced, it is necessary that I have those records to refer to in order to find out names of dead, from whose headboards all marks of identity are obliterated.

—1st Lt. Henry C. Ward, A.A.Q.M., July 15, 1871[1]

The identification of the dead can be lost to time due to the impermanence of the materials used for marking gravesites. Nineteenth-century photographic and documentary evidence from the United States Army's post cemetery at St. Augustine, Florida, show the early use of wooden headboards and the effects of Florida's subtropical climate on the inscriptions. The deterioration of materials and lack of complete and accurate burial registers allowed the corresponding names of the dead to be lost. The unknown graves were eventually marked with small blocks of coquina stone labeled with Roman numerals.[2]

Although standardized marble headstones began to replace headboards in other parts of the country after 1873, it was not until the early 1900s that the coquina blocks marking St. Augustine National Cemetery's unknown graves were replaced by marble headstones.[3] By then, the names of the men in sixty-eight graves were lost, as was the conflict associated with those men.

The erasure from the cemetery of these soldiers' identities was caused by disregard and neglect. It was a complete erasure as the men were buried under unknown soldier headstones labeled with the wrong war. If not for the photographer who captured an image of the few remaining legible headboards, the knowledge of St. Augustine's Union dead would have been lost and the restoration of their names and the honor they deserve would not have been possible.

HISTORY OF THE CEMETERY

The United States gained Florida from Spain in 1821. Gen. Andrew Jackson became the military governor and divided the newly established Florida Territory into two counties: Escambia in the west and St. Johns in the east. The US Army took control of the Castillo de San Marcos, the St. Francis Barracks, and other military buildings throughout the city of St. Augustine on the eastern coastline of St. Johns County. A small US Army post cemetery was attached to St. Francis Barracks on the southern end of the city during the early territorial period.

National cemeteries, which were established during the American Civil War, were restricted to the burial of Union war dead until Congress passed the Act of March 3, 1873, which provided for "all honorably discharged soldiers, sailors, and marines," to be buried in a national cemetery.[4] The War Department began to establish many of the smaller post cemeteries as national cemeteries, and in 1881, St. Augustine's post cemetery received fourth class designation.[5] The classification system was based on the monthly pay of the superintendent of the cemetery, and fourth class received sixty dollars per month.[6] The gravesites within St. Augustine's cemetery represent both military and civilian burials and the earliest date of death of a known soldier is 1828.[7] The present-day cemetery has a mixture of standard government headstones, private markers, and monuments; however, early in the history of the cemetery, many graves were marked with wooden headboards.

At the conclusion of the Second Seminole War in 1842, the most distinctive features of the cemetery were constructed—three coquina-block pyramids and the Dade obelisk.[8] The pyramids were constructed over the mass graves of soldiers who died during the Indian Wars and these unique pyramids appear in many historical photographs of the cemetery. A stereoscopic view of the cemetery circa 1865 set in motion the research described in this essay (Figure 1).[9] Although the pyramids and obelisk themselves are not the focus of this article, their existence in the stereo-

Figure 1. Photographer unknown, Stereogram of post cemetery at St. Augustine, circa 1865. [Saint Augustine National Cemetery], photograph. Library of Congress, https://www.loc.gov/item/2018671309. Public domain.

gram were crucial to the analysis of the image and the correct identification of the Union Civil War soldiers in this cemetery.

By analyzing this photograph and the headboards visible in the foreground, I argue that the sixty present-day headstones bearing the inscription "Unknown U.S. Soldier Indian Wars in Fla." are Union Civil War soldiers and that nine men's graves are identifiable and locatable.[10]

DISSECTING THE PHOTOGRAPH

Three headboards within the photograph are clearly legible (Figure 2). John W. Adsit and J. M. Hoyt died in October 1862, and Eben Chaney died in March 1863. These men were part of the 7th Regiment of the New Hampshire Volunteers (NHV), which was stationed in Florida as an occupying force during the Civil War. By investigating this regiment, names on other eroded headboards within the photograph were deciphered.[11]

The 7th NHV Regiment left Manchester, New Hampshire, on January 14, 1862, and the health of the regiment suffered throughout the period between deployment and arrival in St. Augustine in September 1862. The New Hampshire adjutant general's report of 1865 described the situation:

Figure 2. Legible headboards for John W. Adsit, J. M. Hoyt, and Eben Chaney. Public domain.

> In camp in New Hampshire until mid-winter, then confined in the bad air and straightened limits of a building in New York City, then in the more confined limits of transports until they arrived within a tropical region, the men became weakened and susceptible to disease. Remaining there until the 16th of June, they were transferred to malarious regions, so that they reached St. Augustine in September, having lost by discharge and disease two hundred men. In that period, also, the regiment performed a very great amount of labor for the Government in policing and putting in order forts and garrisons, and in erecting piers, building boats, and doing other government work. In all that time also it was under a severe discipline, and constant drill and instruction. The only approximation to active operation in which any part of the regiment participated, was the movement against Charleston in March 1863, to which Col. Putnam with five companies was attached. But the troops did not disembark from the transports at Folly Island, and the five companies were returned to St. Augustine after an absence of two weeks.[12]

Between their arrival in St. Augustine in September 1862, and their ultimate departure in March of 1863, the regiment lost twenty men. Table 1 lists the soldiers from the 7th NHV who died while stationed in

St. Augustine. Of those with completely legible headboards, John W. Adsit and J. M. (James) Hoyt died early in the assignment, and Eben Chaney was the last of this regiment to die in St. Augustine.

Table 1. List of 7th New Hampshire Volunteers Dying in St. Augustine (in death date order)[a]

Count	Surname	Given Names	Co.	Death Date
1	Sanders	Ivory O.	A	September 17, 1862
2	Gile	William Warren	A	October 3, 1862
3	Hoyt	James M.	K	October 5, 1862
4	Adsit	John W.	K	October 8, 1862
5	Dore	Thomas L.	G	October 18, 1862
6	Darrah	Clinton A.	A	October 24, 1862
7	Harris	Michael	K	October 24, 1862
8	Davis	Randall A.	B	October 28, 1862
9	Durgin	John	G	November 1, 1862
10	McSorley	James	B	November 3, 1862
11	Rowe	John F.	A	November 6, 1862
12	Dana	Anthony	B	November 15, 1862
13	Fisher	John	F	November 20, 1862
14	Wright	Nathaniel	H	November 27, 1862
15	Taylor	Willis J.	B	December 15, 1862
16	Pierpont	William H.	D	December 24, 1862
17	Conner	Parker D.	E	December 26, 1862
18	Grimston	Henry E. S.	A	January 7, 1863
19	Taylor	Franklin A.	B	February 17, 1863
20	Chaney	Eben	F	March 10, 1863

[a] Within this list are two soldiers, Thomas L. Dore and John Durgin, whose presumed resting places within the cemetery were identified in 1918 and presently have headstones with their names.

Six of these men from the 7th NHV are identifiable in the photograph in addition to Adsit, Hoyt, and Chaney. They are Clinton A. Darrah, Anthony Dana, John Fisher, Parker D. Conner, Henry E. S. Grimston, and Frank A. Taylor. The typical pattern of lines on the headboards from top to bottom are rank, name, company and regiment, the word "died" either with the date or on a separate line, the date of death, and the age at death in years. Various parts of these lines on the six other headboards are decipherable and are detailed below.

In addition to the photograph, 1st Lt. William Logan, of the 7th US Infantry and chief quartermaster of the District of Florida, submitted a report on July 5, 1867, entitled "Report of United States Soldiers Who Have Died or Have Been Killed in Action and Interred at the Cemetry [*sic*] of Saint Augustine, District of Florida." The report lists the legible text on the headboards at the time of Logan's visit approximately two years after the stereogram was taken.[13] This list is significant in several ways. First, in comparing the entries on the list with the soldiers from the 7th NHV, it is noted that the order of the list parallels the headboards in the photograph and infers the order in which Logan walked the cemetery. Additionally, the mistakes in the list and the omitted names imply that he was reading deteriorated headboards and deciphered what he could. Table 2 lists the 7th NHV soldiers in the Logan report along with the report's numbering system. Six names, three companies, and seven dates had errors in the transcriptions for this regiment.[14] Additionally, four names were not on the Logan report including two whose deteriorated headboards appear in the photograph (Fisher and Grimston).

Table 2. List of 7th New Hampshire Volunteers from the Logan Report (underlined differences)

Logan #	Surname	Given Names	Co.	Death Date
6	Sanders	Ivory O.	A	September 17, 1862
7	McSartey	James	B	October 3, 1862[a]
8	Gile	William W.	A	October ~, 1862[b]
9	Dore	Thomas S.	~[c]	October 18, 1862
11	Hoyt	J. M.	K	October 5, 1862
12	Adsit	John W.	K	October 5, 1862[d]
13	Darral	Clinton A.	A	October _4, 1862[e]
14	Harris	Michael	K	October 25, 1862[f]
15	Davis	R. A.	~[g]	September 28, 1862[h]
16	Duxgin	John	G	November 2, 1862[i]
17	Rowe	John F.	A	November 6, 1862
18	Dana	Anthony	B	November 15, 1862

(*continued*)

Table 2 (*cont.*)

Logan #	Surname	Given Names	Co.	Death Date
19	Chancy	Eben	F	March 10, 1863
20	Taylor	William J.	B	December 15, 1862
21	C.	P. D.	B	December 26, 1862
22	Taylor	Frank A.	B	February 17, 1863
Not on Logan Report				
	Fisher	John	F	November 20, 1862
	Wright	Nathaniel	H	November 27, 1862
	Pierpont	William H.	D	December 24, 1862
	Grimston	Henry E. S.	A	January 7, 1863

[a] James McSorley died in November.
[b] The day was missing from the list for Gile. There is a tilde shaped character for the day on the list. It does not match the ditto marks used in the other columns and therefore was interpreted as being illegible.
[c] The company contains a tilde for Dore.
[d] John W. Adsit died on October 8th.
[e] Clinton A. Darrah died on October 24th.
[f] Michael Harris died on October 24th.
[g] The company contains a tilde for Davis.
[h] Randall A. Davis died in October.
[i] John Durgin died November 1st.

The six deciphered headboards and the men whose graves they marked are listed below along with the evidence for the identification. Each of the associated figures has side-by-side portions of the stereogram; the left side modified to highlight the deciphered lettering and the right side as the original, unenhanced image.[15]

Clinton A. Darrah

Clinton A. Darrah, James M. Hoyt, and John W. Adsit died within three weeks of each other in October 1862. The headboard to the left of John W. Adsit is dark and shadowed in the photograph; however, there are portions of the image that help to identify the headboard as that of Clinton A. Darrah (Figure 3). The top line's last three letters are clearly "ATE" for his rank of private. The second line is for the soldier's name and begins with "Cl" and has "rr" toward the end. Clinton Darrah is the only soldier in this regiment with a given name beginning with those letters and

Figure 3. Headboard of Clinton A. Darrah, October 24, 1862. Left image enhanced with white lettering. Public domain.

having a double-r in the surname among the Union soldiers identified in this research who died in St. Augustine between 1862 and 1867. The third line ends in "NHV" and the last line (typically the line for death) begins with the word "Died" followed by an uppercase "O" which corresponds to O[ct]. Darrah died on October 24, 1862.

On the Logan report, Clinton A. Darral is listed just after J. M. (James) Hoyt and John W. Adsit (Figure 4), implying Logan walked from south to north along that row of headboards.[16] The "l" on the end of Logan's transcription corresponds to the vertical stroke of a lowercase "h" where the last part of the letter had deteriorated. Logan also misread Darrah's date of death and recorded it as October 4th versus the 24th.

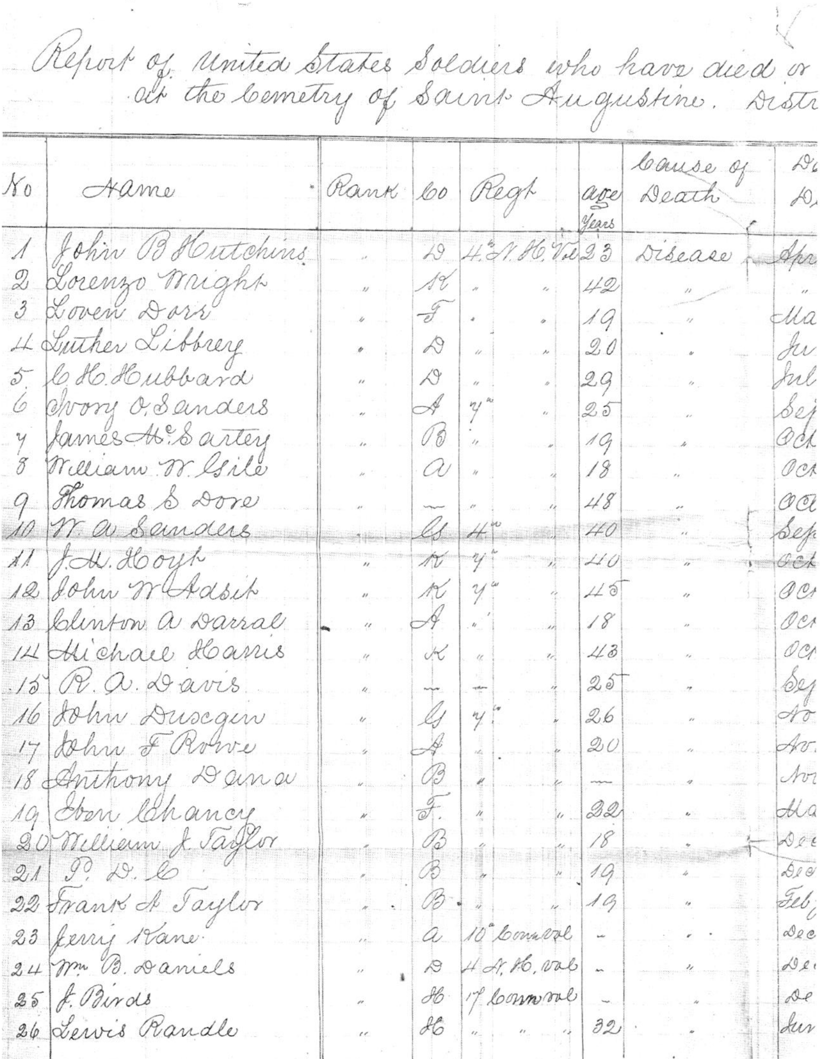

Report of United States Soldiers who have died or
At the Cemetery of Saint Augustine. Distr

No	Name	Rank	Co	Regt	Age Years	Cause of Death	Da D
1	John B Hutchins	"	D	4th N.H. Vol	23	Disease	Apr
2	Lorenzo Wright	"	K	" "	42	"	"
3	Loren Dorr	"	F	" "	19	"	Ma
4	Luther Libbrey	"	D	" "	20	"	Ju
5	C H Hubbard	"	D	" "	29	"	Jul
6	Ivory O. Sanders	"	A	7" "	25	"	Sep
7	James McCartey	"	B	" "	19	"	Oct
8	William W. Cile	"	A	" "	18	"	Oct
9	Thomas S Dore	"	—	" "	48	"	Oct
10	W A Sanders		C	4"	40	"	Sep
11	J.H. Hoyt	"	K	7" "	40	"	Oct
12	John W Adsit	"	K	7" "	45	"	Oct
13	Clinton A Darral	"	A	" "	18	"	Oct
14	Michael Harris	"	K	" "	43	"	Oct
15	R. A. Davis	"	—	—	25	"	Sep
16	John Duscgin	"	C	7" "	26	"	No
17	John F Rowe	"	A	" "	20	"	No
18	Anthony Dana	"	B	" "	—	"	Nov
19	Eben Chancy	"	F	" "	22	"	Ma
20	William J Taylor	"	B	" "	18	"	Dec
21	P. D. C	"	B	" "	19	"	Dec
22	Frank A Taylor	"	B	" "	19	"	Feb
23	Jerry Kane	"	A	10th Conn Vol	-	"	Dec
24	Wm B. Daniels	"	D	4 N.H. Vol	-	"	De
25	J. Birds	"	H	17 Conn Vol	-	"	De
26	Lewis Randle	"	H	" "	32	"	Jun

Figure 4. Portion of Logan's Report including 7th New Hampshire Volunteers. "Report of United States Soldiers Who Have Died or Have Been Killed in Action and Interred at the Cemetry [*sic*] of Saint Augustine, District of Florida," July 5, 1867, General Correspondence and Reports Relating to National and Post Cemeteries ("Cemetery File"), 1865–circa 1914, Quartermaster General's Office, RG 92, entry 576, Box 61, National Archives, Washington, DC. Public domain.

Anthony Dana

When the stereograph was taken, the headboard for Anthony Dana was split between the two halves of the glass plate. His complete headboard is not visible but the portions on either side of the plate have text to identify him (Figure 5).[17] The beginning of the name line on the left plate has the letters "An" visible; on the right plate are the letters "hony," which are the end of "Anthony." Below the name is "Co. B," the company in which Dana served. No other soldier identified during this research is named "Anthony."

In between Clinton A. Darrah and Anthony Dana on the Logan Report are Michael Harris, R. A. (Randall) Davis, John Durgin (misspelled as Duxgin on the report), and John F. Rowe (Figure 4). There are headboards, presumably with text on the back side, in the photograph between the Darrah and Dana rows that could be for some of these men. The pattern of Logan's presumed steps going south to north along each row is shown in Figure 6 oriented to the headboards in the photograph. The camera's angle and the sliver of Anthony Dana's headboard in the image infers that other headboards were likely to the south.[18]

John Fisher

Headboards were often painted white with black lettering, and some, like John Fisher's, over time exhibited cracks and fissures, also known as crazing (Figure 7). The cracks in the paint make it more difficult to read, but letters are still distinguishable. The name line contains most of the letters of John F[i]sher. The second line for company and regiment is more difficult to read; however, the "NHV" is visible. The word "Died" in between the company line and the date is illegible, but the "N" in "Nov" and the rest of the death date are visible. John Fisher died November 20, 1862.

Fisher is not listed on the Logan report. As his headboard was essentially illegible in the photograph, Logan would likely not have been able to read it by 1867. A headstone order card for John Fisher for the village cemetery in Dover, Strafford County, New Hampshire, has the correct death date of November 20, 1862, and a contract date of November 29, 1862.[19] However, the orders for marble markers did not begin until the 1870s. The contract with D. W. Whitney for providing headstones to the

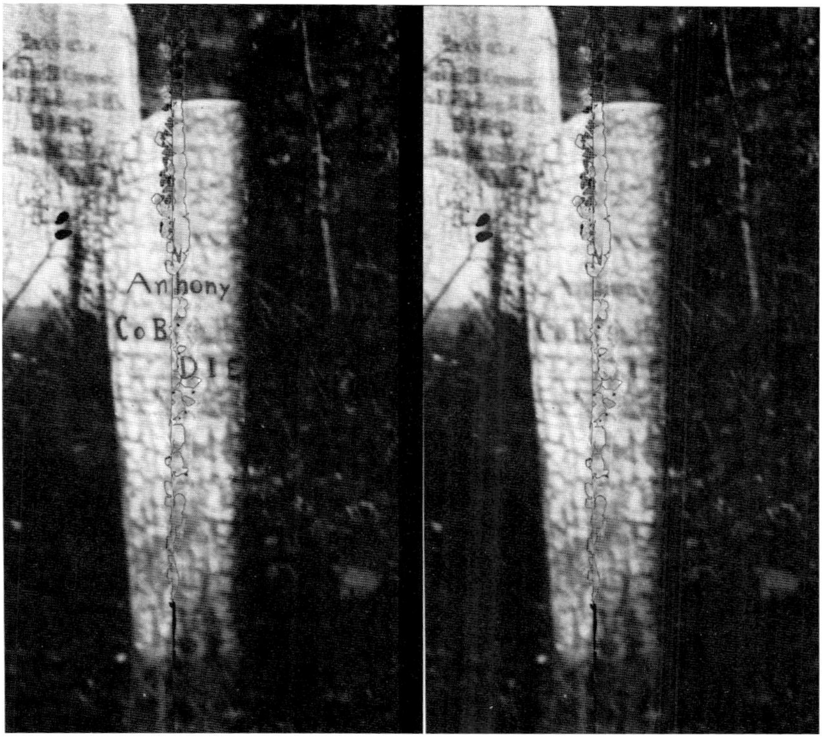

Figure 5. Headboard of Anthony Dana, November 15, 1862. Left image enhanced with black lettering. Public domain.

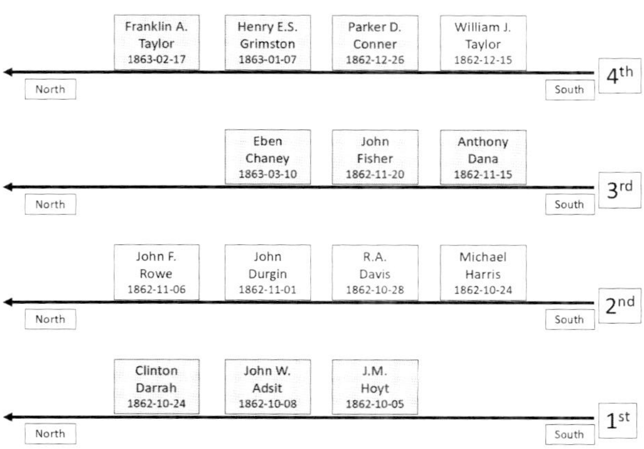

Figure 6. Path of Logan based on order of his report (shaded names are those identified in the photograph).

Figure 7. Headboard of John Fisher, November 20, 1862. Left image enhanced with black lettering. Public domain.

US Army was signed on November 29, 1879, and therefore the 1862 contract date on the order card is likely a transcription error from the original document. Although there is no indication that headstones would be supplied as cenotaphs in private cemeteries, it is unknown when or if Fisher was disinterred and moved to the cemetery in Dover.[20] Typically, a disinterment occurred within months of a soldier's death. The stereogram's estimated date of 1865 would imply that Fisher's remains still rested in St. Augustine three years after his death. Two other men in the 7th NHV who died soon after Fisher have references to their disinterment, one successful and one possibly unsuccessful.

Nathaniel Wright, private, Company H, died on November 27, 1862, Thanksgiving Day. He was from the town of Hollis, New Hampshire. In two letters from Sarah Ann Adams, a woman who lived in Hollis, to her son Charles H. Adams, who served in the 15th NHV, she told Charles of Wright's death and burial. She said, "Nat Wright is dead he died thanksgiving day they have sent for his remains to be sent home" (January 27, 1863) and "I suppose you know that Nathanial Wright is de[a]d his body has be[e]n sent home and was buried last Sunday I suppose that Norman Howe and Charles Fletcher remanes [*sic*] will be brought into town soon" (February 22–23, 1863).[21] Another soldier, Nathanial Truel, mentioned in a letter home that they disinterred Wright on February 6th and sent him home on the steamer *Delaware* the next day.[22]

Almost three months after the death of Fisher, the family of another soldier in the 7th NHV, William H. Pierpont, who had died Christmas Eve 1862, requested that his body be sent home and the surgeon of the regiment, William Whittier Brown, wrote from St. Augustine on February 12, 1863, six days after Wright was disinterred:

> My opinion is that [William's] body would not be received for transportation unless enclosed in a metallic case. We have none here and if we had them, I do not think the amount in the hands of the office large enough to purchase one. The Captains of steamers are not willing to carry bodies unless entirely secluded from the air which we have tried to do and failed with the material we have here, viz—Old hard pine boards torn off from old buildings.[23] [Emphasis original.]

Nothing in the pension file of Fisher's wife, Sarah E. (Cole) Fisher, indicates that he was brought home.[24] Without Fisher on the list, the next name is Eben Chaney and his legible marker in the photograph appears to the left (north) of John Fisher's. Again, Logan would have been walking from south to north between Anthony Dana and Eben Chaney, following the pattern across the grave rows (Figure 6).

Parker D. Conner

Parker D. Conner's headboard is in the furthest row facing the camera in the stereogram (Figure 8). Part of the lower portion is crazed and there is a smaller board (possibly a footboard) in the foreground blocking the last line of text. The "Priv" of private is legible and for the name line, the "P", "D", "C" and the "er" ending "Conner" are visible. The first name is

Figure 8. Headboard of Parker D. Conner, December 26, 1862. Left image enhanced with black lettering. Public domain.

partially obscured by what looks like the branch of a bush or tall grass. The next line begins with "Co. E" and ends with "NHV." The next line is the word "DIED," and the fifth line begins with "Dec" for the month of December with the rest of that line again obscured by the branch/grass. Parker D. Conner was in Company E of the 7th NHV and died on December 26, 1862.

Conner is listed on the Logan report by his initials, P. D. C. No other soldier in the regiment had these initials, and Logan apparently could not decipher the other letters of Conner's names. There is only one name on the Logan list between Eben Chaney and P. D. C. [Parker D. Conner], that of William J. Taylor (Figure 4). Based on the camera's angle, William Taylor could be to the south of Conner. The name following Conner on the list is Frank A. Taylor, brother to William J. Taylor. In the photograph, Frank A. Taylor is two headboards to the north of Conner.

Henry E. S. Grimston

The upper part of Henry E. S. Grimston's headboard is visible behind John Fisher's. It was also cracking, but four lines of the visible text are still partly legible (Figure 9). The top line is Grimston's rank of private. The second line has the "e" and "ry" of the faded name Henry, a darker E. S. for his middle initials, and only the "Grim" of Grimston legible. The line for company and regiment is mostly illegible, but the "A" for his company and the "H" in NHV can be seen. The third line is the word "DIED," and the death date and age are blocked from view by John Fisher's headboard.

Grimston does not appear on Logan's report and this likely indicates that the crazing effaced the rest of the letters in the two years between photograph and report. The next name after Conner on the report is Frank A. Taylor, and this corresponds to the last headboard with writing in the photograph, showing that Logan was continuing his walking pattern by proceeding from south to north along this row (Figure 6).

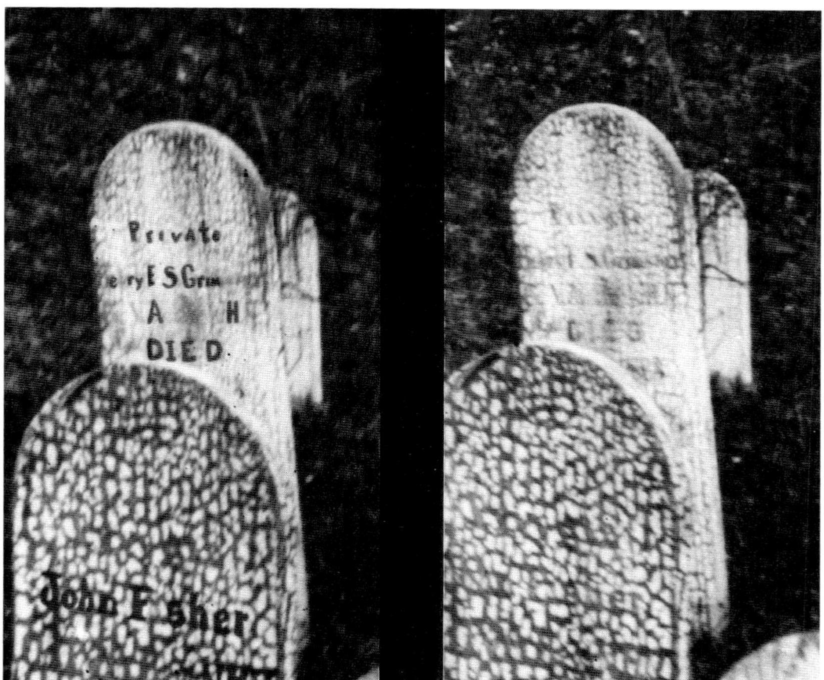

Figure 9. Headboard of Henry E. S. Grimston, January 7, 1863. Left image enhanced with black lettering. Public domain.

Figure 10. Headboard of Frank A. Taylor, February 17, 1863. Left image enhanced with black lettering. Public domain.

Frank A. Taylor

The last headboard with writing is the most difficult to decipher (Figure 10). The first line, which corresponds to rank, appears to begin with "Corp." The second line may begin with "Fr" and have a "Tay" towards the end. The third line begins with "Co. B" and the line ends in "HV" like the other NHVs. The fourth line is "DIED" and the date and age lines are mostly illegible. An "8" can be seen in the year.

Based on death dates and reading from right (south) to left (north) on this row of headboards, there is Parker D. Conner (died December 26, 1862), Henry E. S. Grimston (died January 7, 1863), and Frank A. Taylor (died February 17, 1863). The next month, March 1863, Eben Chaney died and was buried in front (west) of Frank Taylor. The proximity of these headboards, the order of dates of death, the order on the Logan report, and the fact that Frank A. Taylor was the only corporal of the 7th NHV to die in St. Augustine point to this being his headboard. He had been promoted to corporal on February 15, 1863—two days before he died.

The photograph shows the headboards to the south of the pyramids and the nine headboards with visible writing are facing west.[25] Fifteen wooden head/footboards are in the photograph; one marble headstone is to the rear and facing east. In the present-day cemetery, this area has fifteen headstones that are inscribed "Unknown U.S. Soldier Indian Wars in Fla" and where the rectangular headstone stood in the stereogram the present-day headstone corresponds to 1st Sergeant John Williams of the 1st Regiment of Artillery, who died on April 5, 1836, during the Second Seminole War and was buried prior to the erection of the pyramids. His marble marker was erected by his comrades after he was murdered by another soldier.[26]

MISLABELING THE UNKNOWNS WITH THE WRONG WAR

The presence of some individual graves of Florida Indian War dead—those who died and were buried prior to the erection of the pyramids—likely led to the misidentification of the Union graves as those of Indian Wars military personnel. As evidenced by the deterioration visible in the photograph, wood was not a good choice for long-term memorialization of the dead, especially in Florida. Military reports concerning the cemetery noted these issues, including the 1871 letter from 1st Lt. Henry C. Ward to the quartermaster general mentioned in the epigraph.[27] Since Logan had difficulties in 1867 reading the Civil War headboards, it is not surprising that by 1871 some were completely illegible. The focus of the cemetery was the soldiers; typically, the civilian burials and the unknowns were not included in the early burial lists.

A map was created in 1881 for the cemetery's transition to national cemetery status (Figure 11).[28] The map is not to scale (even though it has a scale on it) and only the soldiers were noted by name. None of the civilians and family members were listed in the legend. Many of the gravesites were numbered with Roman numerals and listed in the legend as unknowns (fifty-two total). Others were marked but not labeled in any manner (that is, the five graves in the southeast section, the grave

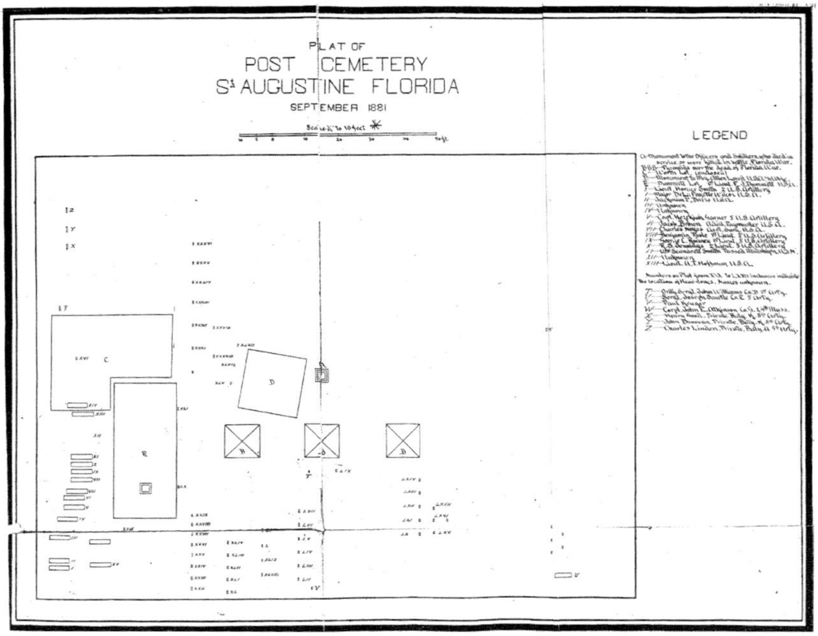

Figure 11. 1881 map of St. Augustine National Cemetery. "Plat of Post Cemetery, St. Augustine, Florida, September 1881," History Program Collection, National Cemetery Administration, Washington, DC. Public domain.

east of III, the grave south of XXXI, and the grave south of LXVI). John Williams' headstone is marked with the letter T and is just south of the center pyramid. Comparing the location of his headstone on the map to that of the stereogram shows the clustering of graves in this area to be skewed farther south on the map than in the photograph.

It was not until the early 1900s that more comprehensive burial lists were created and some effort made to organize the records of the cemetery. The impermanence of wood headboards gave way to coquina blocks of stone to mark the unknown graves (Figure 12).[29] In 1902, the Inspector General's Office wrote to the quartermaster general and noted that "many of the headstones are of coquina rock with only a number on them. They are very perishable and many of them are now crumbling away."[30] In 1905, the decision was made to replace the unknown markers with new marble regulation headstones. The memorandum includes the count and description, "Sixty-eight (68) graves have coquina headstones

Figure 12. Portion of photograph showing coquina marker "LV" near John Williams' headstone, circa 1904. "National Cemetery, St. Augustine, Fla., February 6, 1904," Prints: Photographs of Military Cemeteries in the United States and Mexico, 1873–1912, Alabama–North Carolina, Box 1, Folder 92-CA-4, Office of the Quartermaster General, RG 92-CA, National Archives, College Park, MD. Public domain.

bearing Roman numerals—no record of these on file—supposed to be graves of soldiers killed during Indian wars in Florida."[31]

As the Dade obelisk and the pyramids were dedicated to Seminole War dead, and there were other marked graves of men who died during that war but prior to the erection of the pyramids, those in charge of marking the unknown graves likely surmised that all were from that conflict. Therefore, an order was placed for sixty-eight headstones engraved with "Unknown U.S. Soldier Indian Wars in Fla."[32] At the same time, five headstones engraved "Unknown Indian Prisoner" were ordered for the five unlabeled graves in the southeast section of the cemetery.

On January 2, 1910, David H. Rhodes, landscape gardener and inspector for the national cemeteries, visited St. Augustine National Cemetery and spent days working with the superintendent, George W. Brown, and a laborer, Stafford Kane, trying to correct the burial registers. His report included eleven exhibits, some of which were created prior to his work.[33] Rhodes noted:

> I have understood that former Acting Superintendent, Sergt. Robt. E. Pate, while in charge between 1903 & 1908, put up some 90 headstones at one time to replace the old coquina markers that were formerly used. . . . "Exhibit G" dated January 13, 1903, shows a total of 75 unknown graves, in lieu of 73. . . . Until the time of my visit it seems that the burial register did not contain a single entry of any unknown, and there is nothing on record to show how many unknown have been buried in that cemetery aside from the "proposed identification list," exhibit G, submitted in 1903.[34]

The exhibit to which Rhodes refers is labeled today in red pencil as "H" but is stamped March 16, 1903, and then amended in pen to January 13 (hereafter, referred to as Pate's list). The notations for sixty-nine grave sites are shown as "Unknown—supposed to have lost life in Florida War"; there are five listed as "Unknown—One of the Indian prisoners of Comanche, Kiowa or Arapahoe Bands—about 1874"; and one just listed as "Unknown."[35] This totals the seventy-five which Rhodes mentioned were on Pate's list, and Rhodes' comment "in lieu of" implies that the total should have been seventy-three, the number he found in 1910 (sixty-eight Unknown Florida Wars plus five Unknown Indian Prisoners).[36]

The numbering system on Pate's 1903 list uses a section and number designation. These designations did not completely follow direct rows at the time as the headstones were not precisely aligned, but in general the numbering system started in the southwest corner and the rows ran northward. For example, Section 1 (first row) began with Capt. and Brevet Maj. DeLafayette Wilcox, 5th US Infantry, and ended at the gravesite of Sgt. Adolph Rose, Company L, 2nd US Artillery. Section 2 (second row) included sixteen sequential graves each labeled "Unknown—supposed to have lost life in Florida War." Two headstones from this group of sixteen were subsequently moved in 1909:

> Mrs. Sanno, widow of General Sanno, who also thought that two headstones inscribed "Unknown U.S. Soldier, Indian Wars of Florida", which were placed between the Sprague and Worth graves, were in

> error and that no remains would be found thereat. The superintendent was instructed to excavate the graves and if remains were found to move them to another section of the cemetery. In his report he states that the headstones were removed to either side of Lt. Horace Smith's grave, and that "These two bodies would not interfere with any interments in the Worth plat."[37]

The movement of headstones from their original positions, such as these two being placed over sixty feet away, has complicated the understanding of the original placement of the sixty-eight headstones that were purchased in 1905. Based on recommendations from Rhodes' report, Capt. Charles F. Humphrey, Jr., quartermaster of the Army, sent instructions to the superintendent of the cemetery on March 1, 1912, that included among others, the following items:

> 7. Headstones to be reset so that they will align in both directions, the exact location of the grave (number of inches to the right or left of headstone) to be shown in the "Remarks" column of the burial register.[38]
>
> 10. Identified remains to be transferred where necessary to the perfection of the plan which may be adopted for the rearrangement of the burial sections.
>
> 12. After the graves have been rearranged, proper burial sections established and the headstones reset and realigned, a new system of grave numbers will be established which will give to each section a separate series from 1 up, the sections to be designated by letter.[39]

The rows were aligned and centered by superintendent Roland Osborn, and an alphabetical burial register, which is mostly in Osborn's hand, has the measurements that each headstone was moved. This register also shows the renumbering of gravesites from numeric section and number (Pate's system) to lettered sections (A, B), and instead of restarting at one for each section as instructed, a fully sequential numbering system for the cemetery was used. Only grave sites with known individuals show the renumbering of old to new in Osborn's register. There are two typewritten leaves inserted that record the Unknowns, listing only their new letter and number designation. This unknowns list has a significant change as five of the gravesites formerly with headstones "Unknown U.S. Soldier,

Indian Wars in Fla" are now listed as "Unknown Indian, Florida Wars," leaving sixty-three with the original wording. [40]

In 1912, a typewritten, comprehensive list of the cemetery including vacant grave sites showing the renumbering from one to 687 inclusive was likely created by Osborn from his handwritten list.[41] Like Pate's list, the numbering system began in the southwest corner. This 1912 list includes sixty-four grave sites designated "Unknown U.S. Soldier, Indian Wars in Fla" (one more than Osborn's typewritten inserts), and five headstones, those at the head of the second row, with Osborn's designation of "Unknown Indian, Fla. Wars." This total of sixty-nine mislabeled unknowns from the Florida Wars matches Pate's total. By the 1910s, it is clear that no one knew that these graves were from the Civil War time period, and it is currently unclear why these five gravesites were suddenly designated as Indians. No known documentation describes the reason for this change in the burial lists. It is unknown whether Osborn's was a transcription error from some handwritten list that was replicated or whether those five headstones were replaced with new ones bearing that inscription. Further research may uncover if the change was deliberate or accidental, but it impacts the current argument of this paper as there are sixty-eight Union Civil War soldiers likely buried in the cemetery that match to the count of sixty-eight original "Unknown U.S. Soldier, Indian Wars in Fla." headstones.

IDENTIFYING THE UNKNOWNS

After analyzing the stereogram and concluding that the gravesites to the south of the pyramids were Union soldiers instead of Florida Indian War dead, the new working hypothesis was that the other gravesites marked as Unknown Indian War soldiers were also Union Civil War men. The question then became, could they be identified?

The Logan report, as mentioned previously, lists forty-two Civil War men buried in what is now St. Augustine National Cemetery. In addition to the sixteen 7th NHV soldiers listed on the report, there are twenty-five soldiers from other regiments and one guide who assisted the 17th Connecticut. The list of twelve regiments mentioned on Logan's list include 4th NHV, 7th NHV, 10th Connecticut, 17th Connecticut, 75th Ohio, 9th

Maine, 24th Massachusetts, 40th Massachusetts, 89th New York, 112th New York, 39th Illinois, and the 7th US Infantry. Not all of these regiments served in St. Augustine; men were sent from other posts to convalesce at the hospitals. [42]

The search for soldiers who died in St. Augustine began with researching the men on the Logan list and the regiments in which they served, looking for other men in those regiments whose headboards may have been illegible by Logan's visit. The record groups in which those men were found, such as *Register of the Sick & Wounded, U.S.A. General Hospitals* for Florida,[43] *Returns from U.S. Military Posts, 1800–1916,*[44] and *Registers of Deaths of Volunteers, compiled 1861–1865,*[45] were then searched—in many cases line-by-line—looking for others who fit the criteria. Once a soldier was identified as a potential St. Augustine burial, compiled military service records and pensions (where applicable) were obtained to help verify the place of death. Research identified at least ninety soldiers who died in St. Augustine during and just after the Civil War.[46] Some, like Lt. Oliver H. Walker, were taken directly home for burial,[47] while others, such as Nathaniel Wright, were initially buried in the post cemetery before being disinterred and sent home.

THE REMAINING HEADSTONES

Today in St. Augustine National Cemetery there are only sixty headstones remaining from the 1905 order. One of the missing "Unknown" headstones was replaced in 1918 with one that contained the name of a soldier reputed to be buried in that location. In a letter from superintendent Theodore W. Brake to the quartermaster general, Brake describes an encounter with an elderly member of the 7th NHV:

> Mr. John S. Colbath, formerly of Co. G, 7th N.H.V. Inf . . . called at this cemetery in April 1917, and asked me if I had a record of the interment of John Durgin, private Co. G, 7th N.H. Vols. and of private Thomas L. Dore, of the same company and regiment, who died at this post in November 1862. I looked over my record and informed him no such names were therein; He said, "well they are buried in this cemetery, for I buried both of them and can show you the spot,"

> I went with him to the cemetery and he walked right to a point in section B, where graves Nos. 501 & 502 are, and said the two men are buried right here." One of the graves is now marked with headstone, "U.S. Soldier, Unknown". The other is not marked, but the grave is there all right, as it shown upon the surface. . . . I am so fully convinced that grave No. 501 is the grave of John Durgin . . . that I will recommend that a headstone be furnished for that grave. Also, I will recommend that a headstone be furnished for grave No. 502, now marked "Unknown U.S. Soldier", and that a headstone be furnished for Thomas L. Dore.[48]

Colbath's memory from fifty-five years in the past of where Durgin and Dore were buried can be questioned since the landscape of the cemetery changed radically in that time with headboards being replaced with headstones and rows aligned and centered.[49] Durgin and Dore were both on Logan's list. Dore, who died October 18, 1862, was number nine on the list, two names prior to Hoyt, and therefore likely to the southwest of Hoyt's row and out of the view of the camera. Durgin, who died November 2, 1862, was number sixteen between Clinton Darrah (number thirteen) and Anthony Dana (number eighteen) and therefore in the cluster south of the west pyramid (Figure 7). The graves Colbath identified are to the east of the eastern pyramid and therefore unlikely to be the actual graves of these two men.

From the sixty-eight original headstones, five were involved with the change to Unknown Indian (A-35 through A-39), one was broken and replaced with just "Unknown U.S. Soldier" (A-45), one was replaced with Dore's headstone (B-502), and one (A-230) is now the headstone of John Carey, who was interred on May 19, 1918, leaving the sixty remaining.

Although the Quartermaster General's Office tried their best to maintain the cemetery and its records, it is understandable that assumptions about the conflict (the Second Seminole War versus the Civil War) were based on the surrounding graves and monuments dedicated to the Florida Wars.[50] In examining the clustering of the unknown graves throughout the cemetery, it is conceivable that the burials from 1862 through 1867 were arranged roughly by regiment as shown by the group of 7th NHVs south of the pyramids.[51] Through careful analysis of the stereogram of the cemetery, it clearly shows burials from the Civil War occupy the gravesites currently labeled as "Indian Wars in Florida" dead. These graves have been mislabeled for over 120 years, and through this research, the identities of Union Civil War soldiers who died in St Augustine and were buried in the cemetery are no longer lost to time.[52]

Amy Larner Giroux, PhD, is associate director emerita of the Center for Humanities and Digital Research at the University of Central Florida. Her research involves the contact zone between humans and technology within the intersections of history and learning. By leveraging technologies such as augmented reality and virtual reality, she brings learning to both classroom and field. Her specialty is cemetery research, and she is involved in recording the physical aspects of the spaces through technology such as drone photogrammetry and 360° imagery while also researching the lives of those interred through genealogical research as she is a board-certified genealogist. Her research in St. Augustine National Cemetery has brought to light new information on Civil War soldiers, Native American prisoners of war, and Seminole War history.

Acknowledgments

I would like to thank the anonymous reviewers and editors at *Markers* for their suggestions on this essay. I would also like to thank Barbara Gannon, Jennifer Perunko, and Bryce Carpenter for their support and their belief in the importance of this work.

Notes

1. 1st Lt. Henry C. Ward, A.A.Q.M. to Quartermaster General, United States Army, July 15, 1871, Document File 359,656, Office of the Quartermaster General, 1800–1914, RG 92, National Archives, Washington, DC.
2. "Extract from Report of an Inspection of the St. Augustine, Fla., National Cemetery, made January 25, 1905, by Major Hamilton Rowan, Acting Inspector General" and endorsements, stamped May 4, 1905, Document File 162,331, Office of the Quartermaster General, 1800–1914, RG 92, National Archives, Washington, DC.
3. National Cemetery Administration, "History of Government Furnished Headstones and Markers," US Department of Veterans Affairs,

https://www.cem.va.gov/history/hmhist.asp. As late as 1948, St. Augustine National Cemetery was still using wooden headboards as temporary markers while awaiting shipment of permanent marble headstones, "Records of Expenditures Beginning July 1st, 1942, St. Augustine National Cemetery," entry for Project P311–08, November 8, 1948, 72, Bond-Howell Lumber Co., $28.00 for 35 cedar headboards 30″ x 9″ x 1¼″, Jacksonville National Cemetery, Jacksonville, Florida.

4. Edward Steere, "Expansion of the National Cemetery System, 1880–1900," *Quartermaster Review* 33, no. 2 (September–October 1953): 134.
5. General Orders No. 86, Adjutant General's Office, December 7, 1881, History Program Collection, National Cemetery Administration, Washington, DC, "The post cemetery at St. Augustine, Florida, is announced as a national cemetery of the fourth class, and will be known as the St. Augustine National Cemetery." See also National Cemetery Administration, "Saint Augustine National Cemetery," US Department of Veterans Affairs, https://www.cem.va.gov/cems/nchp/staugustine.asp.
6. War Department, *Compilation of Laws, Orders, Opinions, Instructions, etc., in Regard to National Military Cemeteries* (Washington, DC, 1878), 29–30.
7. Horace Smith, Section A, grave 21, died January 8, 1828, and J[ackman] J. Davis, Section A, grave 3, died February 20, 1828. Death dates were not inscribed on most of the earlier headstones in this cemetery. The civilians are typically family members of military personnel who are also buried in this cemetery. However, some, such as Mrs. West and the Clayton child (d. 1900), do not have obvious relatives in the cemetery. See "Filling in the Blanks: Identifying Mary and Sweet Baby James," *Florida Genealogist* 43, nos. 1 & 2 (2020): 7–18; and "'A sweet and happy child and sunshine in my home'—The Custody Battle for the Clayton Orphans," *Florida Genealogist* 47, no. 1 (June 2024): 6–17.
8. Coquina is a sedimentary rock made primarily of seashells. It was used for construction of buildings in northeast Florida, including Fort Marion (present-day Castillo de San Marcos) and Fort Matanzas south of St. Augustine. The Dade obelisk was erected in 1844.
9. The sleeves containing the two halves (LC-B811–3558A—left and LC-B811–3558B—right) of this glass plate negative are labeled "Soldiers Graves, Savannah, Ga." The Library of Congress has titled the catalog entry as "[Saint Augustine National Cemetery]." The two halves of the original stereogram were recombined digitally for this image. [Saint Augustine National Cemetery], 1865, photograph, Library of Congress, https://www.loc.gov/item/2018671309.
10. James Deal, Reia Drucker, Daniel Foster, and Jordan Richards, "Stereogram Depth Analysis," University of Central Florida Computer Science Senior Design I and II, Fall 2021–Spring 2022. After the author identified the nine soldiers, these undergraduate students used computational and computer

stereo vision methods to calculate the distances in 3D from the corners of the center pyramid to the individual headboards to determine the present-day burial locations and the corresponding modern headstones. For information on these concepts, see Perry E. Borchers, *Photogrammetric Recording of Cultural Resources* (National Park Service, 1997), 20–36; Ebroul Izquierdo, "On the Epipolar Geometry in Stereo Vision," in *Proceedings of the 3rd International Conference on Approximation and Optimization in the Caribbean* (Puebla, Mexico, October 1995); and Charles Loop and Zhengyou Zhang, "Computing Rectifying Homographies for Stereo Vision," in *Proceedings of the IEEE Computer Society Conference on Computer Vision and Pattern Recognition*, vol. 1 (Fort Collins, Colorado, 1999), 125–31.

11. Muster-in Roll service cards for men in the 7th New Hampshire Volunteers note that the regiment became the 7th New Hampshire Infantry.
12. *Report of the Adjutant General of the State of New Hampshire, Year Ending May 20, 1865*, vol. 1 (Concord, NH, 1865), 640–41.
13. "Report of United States Soldiers Who Have Died or Have Been Killed in Action and Interred at the Cemetery [*sic*] of Saint Augustine, District of Florida," July 5, 1867, General Correspondence and Reports Relating to National and Post Cemeteries ("Cemetery File"), 1865–circa 1914, Quartermaster General's Office, RG 92, entry 576, Box 61, National Archives, Washington, DC.
14. Names: McSorley, Dore, Darrah, Durgin, Chaney, and Conner.
15. The Library of Congress has high-resolution files of this image: https://www.loc.gov/item/2018671309. The modified images were manipulated in software to trace over the deciphered letters and highlight them in a contrasting color.
16. The legible headboards in the stereogram face to the west with the burial behind—or to the east—of the headboard.
17. At some point in the past, the original glass plate held at the Library of Congress was cut in half. The image for the visible portion of the headboard was combined from the separate halves of the glass plate images.
18. The cemetery is surrounded on the southern half by a low coquina wall. A burial was found outside of the cemetery wall under the street and points towards other possible burials to the south of the stereogram image headboards. David Z. C. Hines, *Charlotte-San Salvador Historic Burial, St. Augustine, FL, August 2007* (C. A. Pound Human Identification Laboratory, University of Florida, 2007).
19. "Card records of headstones provided for deceased Union Civil war veterans ca. 1879–ca. 1903," entry for John Fisher, Co. F, 7th NH Infantry, RG 92, Microfilm publication M1845, image 354, FamilySearch, https://familysearch.org/en/search/catalog/718264.
20. Jno. Fisher, Co. F, 7th NH Inf. headstone, Pine Hill Cemetery, Dover, Strafford Co., New Hampshire, FindaGrave, https://findagrave.com/memorial/182842242. John's parents, Silas and Tamson Fisher are interred in Pine Hill Cemetery, FindaGrave, https://findagrave.com/memorial/134488121.

21. "1863: Sarah Ann Adams to Charles H. Adams," Spared and Shared 5, https://sparedshared5.wordpress.com/2014/03/09/1863-sarah-a-adams-to-charles-h-adams.
22. "Oh This Pen Cannot Describe My Feelings," Our War, https://ourwarmikepride.blogspot.com/2014/04/oh-this-pen-cannot-describe-my-feelings.html.
23. Mary Pierpont, mother's pension certificate no. 123,980, service of Pvt. William H. Pierpont (Co. D, 7th New Hampshire Infantry, Civil War), Fold3.com, https://fold3.com, images 308570474–518; Case Files of Approved Pension Applications of Widows and Other Dependents of Civil War Veterans, 1861–1934, Department of Veterans Affairs, RG 15, National Archives, Washington, DC. Since William H. Pierpont does not appear on Logan's report, perhaps his mother was finally successful in bringing his remains back to New Hampshire. Surname appears variously as Pierpoint.
24. Sarah E. Cole Fisher, widow's pension certificate no. 4,369 service of Pvt. John C. Fisher (Co. F, 7th New Hampshire Infantry, Civil War), Fold3.com, https://fold3.com, images 146922280–352; Case Files of Approved Pension Applications of Widows and Other Dependents of Civil War Veterans, 1861–1934, Department of Veterans Affairs, RG 15, National Archives, Washington, DC.
25. The headboards in the closest row face Charlotte Street, which is approximately 8° south of west (262°). Based on the shadows cast by the headboards the sun is to the southwest, and with the scarcity of leaves on the trees, it is likely midafternoon in winter or early spring.
26. "Returns of the Killed and Wounded in Battles, 1790–1844," entry for John Williams, 1st Regiment Artillery, Fort Marion, image 71, line 62, Ancestry.com, https://ancestry.com/search/collections/3652/. Williams' original marker, also seen in Figure 12, was replaced with a standard military headstone after 1904.
27. 1st Lt. Henry C. Ward, A.A.Q.M. to Quartermaster General.
28. "Plat of Post Cemetery, St. Augustine, Florida, September 1881," History Program Collection, National Cemetery Administration, Washington, DC.
29. "National Cemetery, St. Augustine, Fla., February 6, 1904," Prints: Photographs of Military Cemeteries in the United States and Mexico, 1873–1912, Alabama–North Carolina, Box 1, Folder 92-CA-4, Office of the Quartermaster General, RG 92-CA, National Archives, College Park, MD.
30. Inspector General's Office to Quartermaster General of the Army, November 19, 1902, Document File 162,331, Office of the Quartermaster General, 1800–1914, RG 92, National Archives, Washington, DC.
31. War Department, Memorandum, February 17, 1905, Document File 162,331, Office of the Quartermaster General, 1800–1914, RG 92, National Archives, Washington, DC.
32. "Extract from Report of an Inspection of the St. Augustine, Fla., National Cemetery, made January 25, 1905, by Major Hamilton Rowan, Acting Inspector General" and endorsements, stamped May 4, 1905.

33. D. H. Rhodes to Quartermaster of the Army, January 2, 1910, 14–15, Document file 162,331, Office of the Quartermaster General, 1800–1914, RG 92, National Archives, Washington, DC. A list of exhibits A through K note items created as far back as 1903.
34. D. H. Rhodes to Quartermaster of the Army, January 2, 1910, 6.
35. Burial list labeled Exhibit H, stamped March 16, 1903, amended to January 13, 1903, Document file 162,331, Office of the Quartermaster General, 1800–1914, RG 92, National Archives, Washington, DC. The list contains sixty-nine entries for "supposed to have lost life in Florida War."
36. George W. Brown submitted a report on March 1, 1909, that indicated there were seventy-three unknowns with headstones in the cemetery at that time. This equates to the sixty-eight Indian War and five Indian prisoners. War Department form submitted by George W. Brown, March 1, 1909, Document file 252,830, RG 92, National Archives, Washington, DC.
37. E. H. Humphrey to D. H. Rhodes, September 24, 1909, Document file 162,331, Office of the Quartermaster General, 1800–1914, RG 92, National Archives, Washington, DC.
38. Some headstones were moved over six feet.
39. C. F. Humphrey Jr. to "Superintendent," March 1, 1912, Document file 357,364, Office of the Quartermaster General, 1800–1914, RG 92, National Archives, Washington, DC.
40. US Burial Registers, Military Posts and National Cemeteries, 1862–1960, Florida, Saint Augustine, Ancestry.com, https://www.ancestry.com/search/collections/3135/, citing RG 15, National Archives, Washington, DC.
41. Burial list, envelope stamped March 1, 1912, Document file 357,364, Office of the Quartermaster General, 1800–1914, RG 92, National Archives, Washington, DC. The numbering system was further adjusted when graves were moved to allow the walks to be paved.
42. "Report of United States Soldiers Who Have Died or Have Been Killed in Action and Interred at the Cemetry [*sic*] of Saint Augustine, District of Florida."
43. *Register of the Sick & Wounded, U.S.A. General Hospitals for Florida,* Records of the Adjutant General's Office, Field Records of Hospitals, 1821–1912, RG 94, National Archives, Washington, DC.
44. *Returns from U.S. Military Posts, 1800–1916,* Records of the Adjutant General's Office, 1780s–1917, RG 94, National Archives, Washington, DC, NARA microfilm publication M617.
45. *Registers of Deaths of Volunteers, compiled 1861–1865,* Records of the Adjutant General's Office, 1780s–1917, RG 94, National Archives, Washington, DC.
46. John Leonard, who died in 1867, is included as he was on Logan's list and would be among the unknowns.
47. "Funeral of Lieut. Walker," *Boston Morning Journal,* January 21, 1864, https://genealogybank.com.

48. Theodore W. Brake to Quartermaster General of Army, February 23, 1918, Entry NM81, 293.7, Office of the Quartermaster General, 1800–1914, RG 92, National Archives, Washington, DC.
49. Grave 502 is not shown as an Unknown headstone on Osborn's list and both 501 and 502 are shown as vacant on the 1912 typed list. The nearest headstone bearing the "Unknown U.S. Soldier, Indian Wars in Fla." phrase would have been B-498 and that headstone is still in place today. Pate's list has a single "Unknown" (non-Indian War designated) line in section 23 next to Hattie Bell George, but the 1912 typed list shows all around her as vacant.
50. Ward, Logan, Rhodes, Pate, Osborn, Brake, and others from the Quartermaster General's Office worked with incomplete records and deteriorated markers. Their efforts, however, allowed this research to be successful.
51. Pvt. John B. Hutchins, Co. D, 4th NHV was the first identified burial during the war, dying April 13, 1862. The last during the war was Pvt. Thornton Gales, Co. K, 34th U.S.C.I., who died December 29, 1865. The last noted by Logan was Cpl. John Leonard, Co. K, 7th US Infantry, who was murdered on February 18, 1867.
52. St. Augustine National Cemetery is on the National Register of Historic Places and therefore, replacement of the physical headstones is restricted. The author is working with the National Cemetery Administration to determine how to acknowledge this history in an appropriate manner in the cemetery.

Frontispiece. Gravestone with a cypress tree motif, Eyüp Mosque graveyard, 2023. Photograph by the author.

"A Cypress Tree for Each Dead"

The Unique Gravemarker in Istanbul's Skyline and Visual Urban Representations

F. İkbal Sezen Polat

CYPRESS TOWER

A peculiar structure in Matthäus Merian's renowned 1635 panorama captured my attention while researching the ancient land walls of Istanbul and tracing their imprints in the city's visual representations (Figure 1). From amid the walls, a towering multi-story edifice stood, crowned with a dense canopy of cypress trees. As an architectural historian, I was surprised by my own unfamiliarity with this prominent structure, which must have either crumbled over time or faded into obscurity, as it was absent from the contemporary cityscape. Scouring my sources, I found no mention of such an edifice. I briefly wondered whether the artist had infused a touch of his own imagination into the city's skyline.

It was only upon noticing that this building was numbered and described in the panorama's legend that a clue emerged: "a walled garden of cypress trees."[1] Moreover, in other versions of Merian's view, different iterations of this depiction appear, each assigning a unique label for the structure: "a masonry of the tree garden with cypress trees,"[2] "a cypress forest built on pillars,"[3] and sometimes described as a tower—"a cypress garden built on towers" (Figure 2).[4]

Ironically, it was my ongoing research into Istanbul's cemeteries, rather than architectural history per se, that provided an answer. To verify this hypothesis, I turned to Melchior Lorck's 1559 panorama, renowned for its precision and lifelike detail (Figure 3). There it was—the

Figure 1. Matthäus Merian (1593–1650), "Ein auffgemaurte garte von cipreßen beumen" (detail), from *Constantinopolis,* circa 1635. Wikimedia Commons. Public domain. https://commons.wikimedia.org/wiki/File:Constantinopolis_-_Matthäus_Merian_-_1635.jpg. https://www.raremaps.com/gallery/detail/52190/constantinopolis-merian.

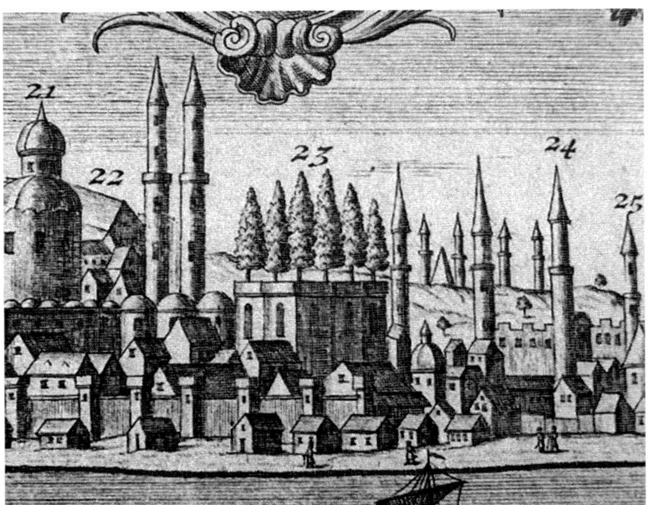

Figure 2. Georg Balthasar Probst (1732–1801) after F. B. Werner (1690–1778), "Ein auf Thürnen gebauter Cypressen garten" (detail), from *Constantinopolis,* eighteenth century. Engraving, on two sheets joined 42x106.5 cm. Copyright Ömer Koç Collection. Published in B. Öztuncay, E. E. Satıcı, and Ş. Çetin., eds., *Istanbul as Far as the Eye Can See: Views Across Five Centuries* (Vehbi Koç Foundation), 190–191. Courtesy of Meşher.

Figure 3. Melchior Lorck (1526/27–1583), Toklu Dede graveyard over the landwalls (detail), from *Prospect of Constantinople*, part 17, 1559. Leiden University Libraries, BPL 1758/17. Public domain. https://digitalcollections.universiteitleiden.nl/view/item/1276353.

same verdant expanse, rendered with greater realism. It was not a grove atop a tower but a green mass nestled between the two layers of the Byzantine land walls. Given my familiarity with the extramural cemeteries beyond the land walls, I recognized the location: it was the Toklu Dede *hazire* (enclosed graveyard).[5] This small burial ground, with its graves and tall cypress trees, occupied the elevated terrain once used for defense between the two trenches of the wall built in the Byzantine era (Figure 4). The towering cypress trees of this Ottoman graveyard had grown to such prominence that a foreign observer from a distant viewing point might have mistaken them for a standalone cypress grove—an apparent architectural novelty, or yet another exotic feature attributed to this non-European city.[6]

This encounter prompted a new question in my ongoing investigation of Istanbul's cemeteries. Could cypress trees reliably signal the presence of cemeteries in the city's skyline and historical visual representations? Might they serve as verdant beacons, revealing hidden graveyards, as in the Merian panorama? Indeed, after an extensive review, I found them prominently featured in panoramas and maps to denote cemeteries.

Figure 4. Interior view of Toklu Dede graveyard, 2022. Photograph courtesy of Fatih Yasin Köroğlu. https://kulturenvanteri.com/tr/yer/toklu-dede-haziresi/#16/41.039295/28.941.

Furthermore, it turned out that they not only marked the cemeteries and helped identify them (to a certain degree), but also eventually became a cartographic symbol for cemeteries.

ISTANBUL'S CEMETERIES: NATURE OR URBAN

The cypress tree has long graced Ottoman cemeteries, even before Istanbul's rise to prominence. Ottoman scholar Godfrey Goodwin named Ottoman cemeteries as "gardens of the dead," elaborating that "the place of the dead is a garden, its dominant feature being the cypress tree."[7] The first part of this sentence attests to the ambiguous spatial character of Ottoman cemeteries, which are often caught in a dichotomy between nature and the urban environment, especially in Istanbul's historiography. Due to their pronounced natural elements—most notably, the cypress trees—these cemeteries are frequently classified as natural landscapes, thereby being overlooked in modern historiography of the built environment. Yet it is precisely the cypress tree that both sustains and unsettles this distinction: while it renders cemeteries seemingly natural, it also operates as a visual and architectural component of the city itself. This tension provides the conceptual ground for understanding the cypress's dual role in Istanbul's urban fabric, a theme explored in the following sections.

For instance, while Maurice Cerasi categorized Ottoman cemeteries as "Urban Open Spaces" alongside parks and gardens in *La Città del Levante*,[8] Reinhold Schiffer's *Oriental Panorama* dedicated a "Cemeteries and Playgrounds" subchapter within "Ottoman Outdoor Recreations."[9] Marcel Bazin's 2008 article, "La nature à Istanbul," also considered cemeteries within this nature-oriented perspective.[10] Goodwin's landmark text, *A History of Ottoman Architecture*, omitted cemeteries entirely.[11] He later addressed them separately in the abovementioned article, defining them as gardens.

Yet, the sheer scale of these "gardens" in Istanbul far eclipses that of any other Ottoman city, rendering them impossible to ignore.[12] European visitors, shocked by their vastness, expressed their astonishment. In 1608, Salomon Schweigger emphasized that everyone had "their own special grave" and that there were "cemeteries all over Constantinople for half a German mile."[13] In 1721, Cornelius Drieschius stated that the cemeteries of Constantinople occupied larger areas than the city itself and the tombstones within them could be used to "build another city." Joseph de Tournefort further commented in 1701 that if the burial areas were planted with corn, the city could be fed for half of the year.[14] He added that a second land wall could be built in the city using their tombstones. The same narrative continued into the nineteenth century, when in 1830 Michaud and Poujoulat expressed their concerns for the living amid this vastness of the dead:

> Since coffins are sacred and one would sooner move a mosque or a palace than a sepulchre, people are constantly forced to open new graves in new plots of land, so that one can no longer tell where the tombs end. I sometimes lose myself in these calculations; I do not see what will become of the living population of this country.[15]

These sprawling cemeteries, encircling the city along its historical boundaries, (outside the Theodosian land walls of the historical peninsula, beyond the Galata walls across Golden Horn and on the fringes of Üsküdar settlement on the Asian side) have most indelibly shaped Istanbul's spatial identity, both in layout and elevation. This enduring impact stems from the fact that burial grounds were permanently inviolable under Islamic religious law.[16]

Although initially established beyond urban confines, communal cemeteries repeatedly meshed with inhabited spaces: Ottoman urban sprawl swallowed the once-outlying cemeteries of Galata, blending Pera into a realm of both the living and the dead (Figure 5).[17] This fusion was also exemplified, in the nineteenth century, when the town of Üsküdar grew beyond its de facto borderline at the Karacaahmet cemetery, where daily life flowed through the veins indented throughout its vast ground (Figure 6). Foreign visitors were particularly struck by the omnipresence of these death-infused spaces within the urban milieu. Antonio Baratta remarked in 1840 that the entirety of Istanbul seemed like "a continuous succession of tombs, necropolises, and mortuary memories."[18] French traveler François-René de Chateaubriand, writing in 1807, observed the juxtaposition of quotidian functions and mortality in the city, noting, "We constantly move from a bazaar to a cemetery—as if the Turks were only there to buy, sell, and die."[19] Especially within the intramural city, the profusion of *türbes* (monumental mausoleums) and *hazires* (enclosed graveyards adjacent to mosques) permeated everyday spaces, with solitary *kabirs* (stand-alone graves) further adding to this urban tapestry of death.[20]

Figure 5. View of Pera cemeteries as dense cypress groves, from Vue 11 of *Très grand panorama photographique de Constantinople monté en album,* nineteenth century. Bibliothèque nationale de France, Département Société de Géographie, SG WC-534. Public domain. https://gallica.bnf.fr/ark:/12148/btv1b10512941j/f11.item.

Figure 6. *Cypresses and road leading to the cemetery, Scutari, Constantinople, Turkey, between circa 1890 and 1900.* Library of Congress Prints and Photographs Division, LOT 13428, no. 005. Public domain. https://www.loc.gov/pictures/item/2001699428/.

Young Charles-Edouard Jeanneret, strolling through the streets of Istanbul—before he became Le Corbusier, the pioneering modernist architect—observed in awe this "urbanness" of cemeteries:

> Istanbul is buried under graves. People love graves. Graves penetrate into the courtyards of houses. . . . Houses are built, trees are planted,

> and people bury their dead in the remaining land. Graves enter the streets, settle under the branches of trees, and in graveyards around mosques; the sultans lie in great tombs, blue thistles grow in this land. A Turk's life begins with a mosque, goes to coffeehouses where tobacco is smoked without talking, and ends in a cemetery.[21]

Melchior Lorck's meticulously detailed panorama from 1559, still largely unacknowledged for its precise depiction of cemeteries in early modern Istanbul, vividly illustrates their dual nature, oscillating between the realms of the natural and the urban.[22] In the foreground, Muslim cemeteries just outside the Galata walls seamlessly meld into the built environment, nestled close to residences, with cypress trees framing their boundaries (Figure 7). Conversely, Tokmaktepe and Eyüp cemeteries located beyond the land walls, seen in the far distance across the Golden Horn, blend almost indistinguishably with the surrounding wilderness, their tombstones sporadically piercing the verdant expanse (Figures 3 and 8).

Returning to the latter part of Goodwin's statement, the cypress tree does not yet emerge as the "dominant feature of cemeteries" in this early modern portrayal of the metropolis. In fact, the relative absence of cypress trees in the then-emerging cemeteries of Tokmaktepe and Eyüp, juxtaposed with their pronounced presence in the older Galata cemeteries, hints at a temporal progression. A nineteenth-century photograph capturing Eyüp cemetery from a viewing angle similar to Lorck's attests to this transformation over time (Figure 9). Danish author Hans Christian Andersen's observation during his 1841 visit to Istanbul further reflects the cultural logic underlying this process: "Turks plant a plane tree for each child born, and a cypress tree for each dead."[23]

CYPRESS TREES AS HUMAN

In 1533, Pieter Coecke van Aelst vividly depicted seven distinct scenes from his journey to Istanbul. Notably, the fifth frame captures a funeral procession (Figure 10). This depiction is meticulous in its detail, spotlighting a rich variety of Ottoman graves and gravestones, even incorporating a Christian tombstone marked by a cross, offering a comprehensive

Figure 7. Melchior Lorck (1526/27–1583), cemeteries around Galata (detail) from *Prospect of Constantinople,* part 13, 1559. The darker shaded regions in the foreground and right background are gravestones marked by the author. Leiden University Libraries, BPL 1758/17. Public domain. https://digitalcollections.universiteitleiden.nl/view/item/1276353.

Figure 8. Melchior Lorck (1526/27–1583), cemeteries over the hill in Eyüp (detail) from *Prospect of Constantinople,* parts 20 and 21, 1559. The darker shaded regions are gravestones marked by the author. Leiden University Libraries, BPL 1758/17. Public domain. https://digitalcollections.universiteitleiden.nl/view/item/1276353.

Figure 9. Sébah & Joaillier, *Constantinople: Mosquée et tombeaux d'Eyoub* [Mosque and tombs of Eyüp], viewed from the Golden Horn at a similar angle to Lorck's panorama, circa 1884. From the Pierre de Gigord Collection of Photographs of the Ottoman Empire and the Republic of Turkey, Series III: Loose and Mounted Photographs, 96.R.14 (C18.2a). The Getty Research Institute, Los Angeles. Public domain. https://rosettaapp.getty.edu/delivery/DeliveryManagerServlet?dps_pid=IE2905181.

Figure 10. Pieter Coecke van Aelst (1502–1550), *A Turkish Funeral from the frieze Ces Moeurs et fachons de faire de Turcz* [Customs and fashions of the Turks], 1553. The darker shaded regions are gravestones marked by the author. Harris Brisbane Dick Fund, 1928. 28.85.5. The Metropolitan Museum of Art, New York. Public domain. https://www.metmuseum.org/art/collection/search/375771.

visual guide for its European audience. Accompanying this visual is a descriptive annotation on Turkish funeral customs. However, instead of elucidating burial practices, van Aelst's commentary centers on the prominence of cypress trees. He describes the cemetery as a verdant grove dominated by these trees and recounts a captivating tradition: "They climb these trees each year looking at all trees and announce the highest tree that surmounted others, thinking, and believing that the soul buried beneath this particular tree is in a place of greater glory than the others whose trees grow less."[24]

Though it remains uncertain whether tree-climbing was a common practice, as visualized by Coecke van Aelst on the left side of the image, the notion appears to have persisted. By the late eighteenth century, John Griffiths observed the planting of young cypress saplings during burial ceremonies. When he inquired about the ritual of planting two trees, one on each side of the grave, he was informed of a folk belief: if the tree on the right-hand side prospers, it augurs peace for the departed soul. If the left one thrives, it portends a denial of peace. Should both trees flourish, it signifies the soul will attain an exceptional place in the afterlife; conversely, their mutual failure means that black angels will torture the soul.[25] Miss Julia Pardoe, in 1836, documented a variation: the cypress trees were positioned at the head and foot of the grave, and if their tops were bent, it was believed to signal that the soul beneath was cursed.[26]

These superstitions, beyond showing the cypress's association with funeral and burial practices, point to a highly common conception of identifying the cypress with the soul of an individual, effectively relating the cypress to the human. Even more so, in the high forms of Ottoman art, mainly *diwan* literature and miniature painting, the cypress tree was frequently employed as a metaphor for the human form. Its characteristics of height and shape were used descriptively: symbolizing the svelte beauty of a lover, praising the slender grace of women, and lauding the sturdiness of men.[27] This simile was the most prevailing, as in Rumi's verses: "Where did the handsome beloved go? / I wonder, where did that tall, shapely cypress tree go?"[28] A miniature painting from 1603 depicting a scene from an Ottoman harem, where a group of women is shown against rows of cypress trees in the background, exemplifies this tradition of mirroring human figures with arboreal forms (Figure 11).[29] Remarkably, in Greek mythology, the cypress tree itself originates from a human. In Ovid's *Metamorphoses*, young Cyparissus kills his beloved stag by mistake and, because of the greatness of his grief he prays to die. Apollo transforms him into a cypress tree at the spot.[30] Even though the myth is often considered as the cypress's association with death and mourning, it is fundamentally a creation myth, inscribing the cypress as emerging from a human body.[31]

In pious Sufi imagination, the cypress tree was revered as sacred, infused with mystical import, often through anthropomorphic associations and parallels to human actions. The rustling sound produced by swaying cypress trees in the wind was lyrically imagined as the trees reciting "*dhikr*" (remembrance of Allah), whispering "*Hu*" (exclamation for Allah) in repetition.[32] The subtle arch of their crowns was interpreted as the trees performing "*sajdah*" (prostration to Allah).[33] A similar metaphor was eloquently echoed by the sixteenth-century poet Hayalî, who likened the cypress to a "dervish" (devoted member of Sufi religious order) in green attire, with the world serving as his sanctuary.[34]

Figure 11. *Haremde Eğlence* [Entertainment at the harem], from the *Album of Ahmed I*, 1603–1614. Topkapı Palace Museum Library, Istanbul, Ms. B.408, f.19a. Filiz Çağman and Zeren Tanındı, *Topkapı Sarayı Müzesi İslam Minyatürleri* (Tercüman Sanat ve Kültür Yayınları, 1979). Public domain. https://www.meisterdrucke.com.tr/fine-art-baski/Ottoman-School/961601/Sultan-I.-Ahmed%27in-%281590-1617%29-albümünden-minyatür-haremde-düzenlenen-şenlikler-17.-yüzyıl-İstanbul-Topkapı-Sarayı-Müzesi-Kütüphanesi.html.

On the other hand, the fact that the cypress tree, often used as a decorative motif in crafts, is widely recognized as the "tree of life"[35] adds another layer of meaning to its symbolic representation of the human. Its evergreen botanical qualities—strength, durability, and resilience—symbolize eternal life, longevity, or immortality in various artistic and architectural contexts.[36] For instance, beside a fountain faucet, it represents the life-giving powers of water (*ab-ı hayat*),[37] while on dynastic clothing, talismanic shirts, or battle shields, it signifies a wish for a long life and protection. In mosque tile decorations, the cypress brings glad tidings of heaven—the eternal life.[38]

Given this spiritual and artistic backdrop, the iconographic meaning of the cypress's frequent appearance on Ottoman gravestones simmers down to human presence—body and soul, and life—earthly and heavenly—expressing the continuity between life and afterlife in Islamic eschatology (Figures 12 and 13). In that sense, the use of the "tree of life" symbol in Ottoman cemeteries is not contradictory; it reflects the belief in one continuous life unfolding in two stages: the mortal body and the immortal soul. As Recep Kankal states: "Cypress is the symbol of man's existence from birth to death and of unity which is becoming one (with God), in Turkish traditions and social beliefs."[39] Indeed, its anthropomorphic attribution on gravestones functioned both ways: to express the individual's bodily and metaphysical conditions. For the former, an overt example is a gravestone made for a pregnant woman, where the depiction of a smaller cypress is encompassed within a larger one.[40] For the latter, a slight nuance in formal depiction sufficed to communicate the character of the individual: the tree's curved silhouette on tombstones was perceived as an embodiment of the deceased's obedience to God—like a person with head bowed—while its upright form signified their honesty and integrity—like a person with head held high.[41]

Figure 12. Gravestone with a cypress tree motif, Eyüp Mosque graveyard, 2023. Photograph by the author.

Figure 13. Gravestones with cypress tree motifs, Eyüp Mosque graveyard and Zal Mahmut Paşa Graveyard, 2025. Photographs by the author.

Notably, while the cypress tree was almost exclusively planted in the Muslim cemeteries of Ottoman Istanbul—with Jewish graveyards completely devoid of any tree flora[42]—rare instances of cypress motifs on Armenian and Jewish tombstones showcase its expansive, cross-cultural resonance in Istanbul.[43] In fact, the cypress tree was used in Istanbul's non-Muslim past, too, in Byzantine cemeteries and death-related contexts. A ninth-century inscription found in Istanbul records the planting of cypress trees in commemoration of the dead: "With the good will of the holy Martyr / And the grace of God these cypress trees / Were planted in the year 6411 to the fair / Memory of Arsavir, the pious imperial / Spatharius and gentleman of the bedchamber."[44]

According to Byzantine historian Cyril Mango, the Ottomans perpetuated the traditions of their Byzantine predecessors, and this record "illustrates the ancient origin of cypress groves in cemeteries."[45] In addition to this, I draw attention to a Byzantine funerary decoration that, to my knowledge, has not previously been recognized for its depiction of cypress trees. A surviving fragment of a fresco that adorns the inner wall of the Silivrikapı Hypogeum (a family tomb) from the seventh century features cypress trees positioned between human figures (Figure 14).[46] Byzantine intellectual Theodore Metochites (1270–1332), born in Constantinople, reflected on the cypress tree as a spiritual example for humankind through its anthropomorphic shape: "'unfruitful' yet 'straight-standing' cypress, 'which in raising even to the skies . . .' proclaims without artifice to those who meditate there the way in which they are to walk and strive upward, laying aside gradually as they go up the excess of their material part and growing thinner as they rise."[47]

The symbolic attributions of the cypress tree in the Ottoman realm were a convergence of both Muslim and non-Muslim cultural influences. While the Turkish name of the tree "*servi*" itself originates from the Persian "*serv*," their ubiquitous presence in Istanbul's "deathscape" echoes Byzantine and, by extension, Greco-Roman influences.[48] In Greek and Roman cemeteries, cypresses were planted in rows between the tombs.[49] In Roman antiquity, the death of a household member prompted the placement of a cypress branch at the doorway. This signaled to visitors or passersby the presence of death.[50] Also, it was used in funeral pyres or placed over grave mounds.[51]

On the other hand, the cypress tree's widespread association with burial and cemeteries throughout the shared past of Byzantine and Ottoman Istanbul was also indebted to its functional value, beyond mere symbolism. The cypress tree held a practical role in burial grounds due to its inherent botanical characteristics. Its potent aroma was capable of masking the inevitable odors emanating from a cemetery.[52] Burning cypress branches during funeral processions in Roman times also attests to this aromatic feature.[53] In a similar vein, an Ottoman state document from 1893 indicates a similar use in funerals, and thus in cemeteries, in relation to health purposes. According to this record, the resin found in the cypress tree was used as incense to disinfect against cholera by taking advantage of its antimicrobial properties and was burned among

Figure 14. Mehmet İ. Tunay, fresco from the Hypogeum of Silivrikapı, 2001. Mehmet İ. Tunay, "Byzantine Archaeological Findings in Istanbul during the Last Decade," in *Byzantine Constantinople: Monuments, Topography and Everyday Life,* edited by Nevra Necipoğlu (Brill, 2001), 219 (*above*). Photograph courtesy of İnci Tunay and Can Tunay. Ivan Foletti, *Silivri-Kapı mausoleum, principal sarcophagus with frescoes on the north wall, sketch of the cross-section,* 2013. Ivan Foletti, "Of Holes and a Holy Man: New Discoveries in the Silivrikapı Mausoleum in Istanbul," *Kunstchronik* 66 (2013): 180 (*below*). Drawing courtesy of Ivan Foletti.

the residents in the neighborhood.[54] Cypress tree-shaped brass incense burners used within Ottoman mausoleums hint at a similar connection (Figure 15).[55]

Ultimately, across myth, art, and religion, the cypress tree functions as a botanical counterpart of the human being. Its growth is linked to the fate of the soul, its form associated with human grace and virtue, and its presence imagined as a sign of spiritual devotion. Its presence on gravestones and in cemeteries thus operates not merely as ornament or symbol, but as a visual and material continuation of the human form itself—standing upright in the place where the body rests, mediating between earth and heaven.

Figure 15. Stationary censer, Museum of Turkish and Islamic Art, Istanbul, no. 18, 1624. Photograph courtesy of Museum of Turkish and Islamic Art.

CYPRESS TREES AS ARCHITECTURE

I propose another role the cypress tree came to play in the unique geographical context of Istanbul: an "architectural" function. While surely not part of a coordinated imperial architectural plan, the cumulative presence of cypress groves over the centuries nonetheless created a vertical rhythm in the city's skyline, echoing—without equating to—the city's towers and minarets. I began exploring this idea after observing Merian's aforementioned depiction of the cypress grove as a tower (Figure 1). Presented as a distinct "building" within the urban fabric, it led me to ponder an analogy between the verticality of cypresses in the cemeteries and the city's tall structures. This included not just modern high-rises, but also the soaring minarets of Ottoman mosques and the monumental columns of the Byzantine period. The visual composition of an allegorical version of Merian's panorama from 1670, in which all vertical structures seem amplified, almost competing in their grandeur, suggests that these cypresses stood purposefully in the city's skyline (Figure 2). In a way, the cypresses provided the vertical dimension to cemeteries, which, in their inherent horizontal spread, might otherwise have faded from the distant observer's eye. In 1899, another European visitor, Knut Hamsun, also imagined Istanbul's cypresses as architecture: "The cypresses are motionless, like upright towers."[56]

Yet, the cypress tree, especially in the form of the dense cypress groves of vast extramural cemeteries, performs an architectural function particularly in Istanbul's specific geographical context. Istanbul's hilly topography offers myriad viewpoints, affording the city its picturesque landscapes, and Istanbulites seem aware of their city's "vistas." This awareness is evident in the strategic placement of imperial mosques on prominent hills and the imperial choice to build the Topkapı Palace on the peninsula's precipice in the fifteenth century. Topkapı Palace's architectural composition, with its balconies and large terraces looking out to views of the Bosphorus, the Asian coastline, and the Golden Horn, reveals an early appreciation of Istanbul's scenic topography. Later in the nineteenth century, Antoine Ignace Melling's engraving titled *View of Uskudar from Pera*, highlights this "viewing" sensibility by displaying at its center people watching the view from a terrace (Figure 16). Directly opposite these viewers, the continuous line of cypresses of grand Karacaahmet cemetery in Üsküdar dominates the horizon. Again, at a very similar

Figure 16. Antoine Ignace Melling, Vue de la ville Scutari prise de Pera [View of Uskudar from Pera] (detail), from *Voyage pittoresque de Constantinople et des rives du Bosphore . . . Collection des planches*, 1819. Salt Research, AMN09902. Public Domain. https://archives.saltresearch.org/handle/123456789/117933?locale=tr.

angle by Philipp Franz Gudenus from the previous century, the same dark line made of cypresses is used as the only signifier of the cemetery listed in its legend. Both these images clearly express the cypress tree's role as the vertical component of cemeteries within the city's skyline in response to anticipated viewing relationships.

The slender design of Ottoman minarets also attests to a deep understanding of urban skylines and the significance of vertical architectural elements. According to renowned architectural historian Spiro Kostof, the minarets demonstrated Ottoman appropriation of Istanbul's skyline.[57] The cypress tree seamlessly fit this architectural vision, often drawing comparisons to the towering minarets in literary tradition.[58] The sixteenth-century poet Hayalî eloquently captures this sentiment: "A nightingale's melodic serenade atop a cypress is / A man reciting the Quran atop a minaret."[59] Remarkably, in several instances, both human body and minaret are converged with the cypress tree metaphor: "If you look, if you watch, each minaret / turns into a lover as tall as a cypress tree."[60] Indeed, cypresses and minarets meld into each other in Cornelis de Bruyn's seventeenth-century panorama, the minarets of the mosque situated behind the Kasımpaşa cemetery becoming indistinguishable from the cemetery's cypress trees (Figure 17).

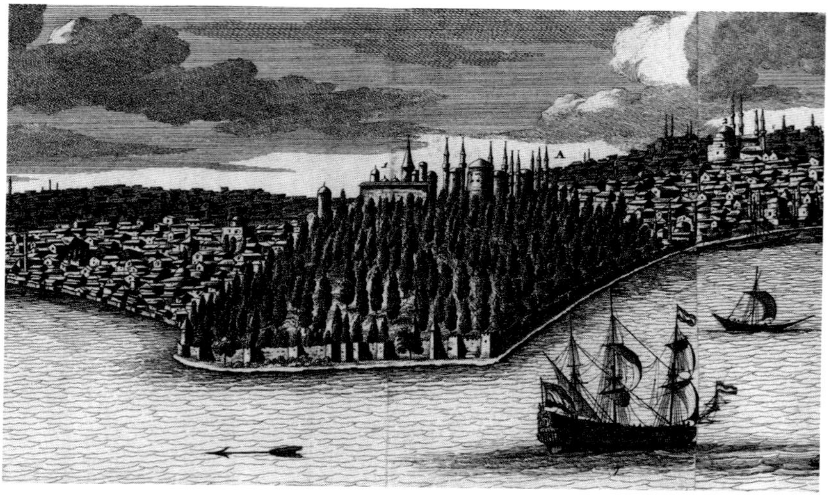

Figure 17. Cornelis de Bruyn (1652?–1727?), Vue 92 (detail), from *Voyage au Levant, c'est-à-dire, dans les principaux endroits de l'Asie Mineure . . .*, 1714. Bibliothèque nationale de France, Département Arsenal, FOL-H-311. Public domain. https://gallica.bnf.fr/ark:/12148/bpt6k1040601r/f92.item.

This architectural interpretation of cypress trees as vertical markers of cemeteries in the city's skyline resonates with the Ottoman societal emphasis on ensuring the visibility of the dead, which is evident in the popularity of *türbe* (monumental mausoleums) as a widespread urban typology in Ottoman cities.[61] These monumental tomb structures, already designed to elevate and thus make the dead more visible within the urban setting, thrived even in the face of discouragement in Islamic jurisprudence against ostentatious displays of the deceased and monumentalizing the dead.[62] As Ottoman architectural historian Gülru Necipoğlu highlights, imperial tombs were strategically interspersed throughout the urban tapestry, especially over hills, serving as visual symbols of imperial authority.[63] This perspective is reiterated by scholars Maurice Cerasi and Edhem Eldem, who respectively suggest that the urban placement and architecture of elite burial grounds within the intramural city were primarily driven by a desire for posthumous public visibility.[64] This aspiration led the high-elite to choose burial sites along Divanyolu Street, the city's major ceremonial route, where tombstones were strategically positioned to face the street for maximum public exposure, even at the expense of traditional burial orientation toward Mecca.

One reason behind this societal phenomenon, the religious aspiration to elicit commemorative prayers from passersby as rooted in Islamic teachings, was not restricted to the elite.[65] This pious fervor prompted the high concentration of gravestones along roadsides in communal cemeteries of ordinary people outside the city walls.[66] In this regard, Miss Julia Pardoe's remarks about the placement of Turkish cemeteries "in the most lovely spots" of the city, especially on hilltops, highlight their positioning that maximizes their visibility within the urban fabric.[67] She attributed what made them distinguishable in the city's silhouette even from a far distance to their cypress groves: "A forest of the finest cypresses extending over an immense space, clothing hill and valley, and overshadowing, like a huge pall, thousands of dead, is seen far off at sea, and presents an object at once striking and magnificent."[68]

The architectural role of cypress trees also operated within a political domain. While Jewish cemeteries were typically devoid of trees, Armenian and Greek burial sites featured varied trees alongside the cypress.[69] The domination of the cypress as the singular plant in most Muslim cemeteries caused an exclusive association of cypresses with Muslim burial grounds, accentuating their presence in the city's skyline. The recognition of the cypress as an Islamic symbol among Ottomans is also reflected in Matrakçı Nasuh's Istanbul map. In this miniature-style map from 1537, he adorned the backgrounds of buildings with cypress trees to signify Muslim domains, while leaving the Galata district, where the non-Muslim population resided, devoid of any.[70] Through this lens of religiopolitical appropriation, the cypress trees of Muslim cemeteries, alongside the minarets, helps transform Istanbul's skyline into a testament of Muslim dominion—through the ancestors who endured in the form of cypress trees.

CYPRESS TREES AS A CARTOGRAPHIC SIGN

The cypress tree's significance in the urban skyline was to the extent that it evolved into a distinctive sign for cemeteries even in two-dimensional cartographic representations. Its architectural role as the vertical component of cemeteries was emphasized in this transition, as its vertical form was consistently preserved in map drawings. Remarkably, cypress trees were shown in elevation view, in their vertical form, across the horizontal plan view of maps, even when the cartographic tradition moved from bird's-eye views to scientific plan views.[71] Tracing back to the earliest known maps of Istanbul, however, there is a stark absence of cypress trees. In the Düsseldorf copy of Cristoforo Buondelmonti's and Giovanni Andrea Vavassore's bird's-eye views showing the city circa 1480–90, the only cemeteries featured in the view are demarcated using just headstones.[72] Several maps from the sixteenth and seventeenth centuries that include cemeteries in their visual program also rely on tombstones as the sole clue of burial grounds. Yet in others, the next stage in cemeteries' cartographic representation appears as the combination of headstones and cypress trees, without an apparent distinction between foreign or Ottoman-made representations.[73]

This combination is evident in The Walters Art Museum's copy of the Istanbul map from *Kitab-ı Bahriye* [Book of navigation], based on the 1526 original by the famous Ottoman naval commander Piri Reis.[74] It highlights Karacaahmet cemetery in Üsküdar with abstracted Ottoman gravestones interspersed with cypress trees in a compellingly clear way, without textual annotation (Figure 18). Comparing this visualization with the other depiction of cemeteries on the same map, rendered as full-grown, dense cypress groves piercing through the city's built fabric, it seems to reflect the different stages of development of these cemeteries at the time.[75] Another early modern Ottoman map to feature a cemetery

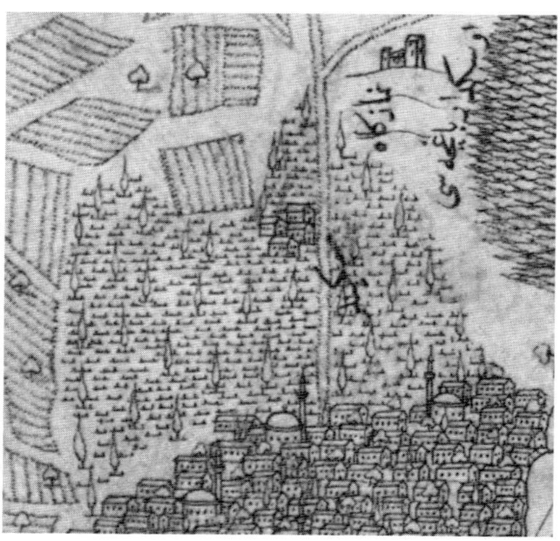

Figure 18. Piri Reis (1465–1555), cemetery of Uskudar (detail) from Map of the City of Istanbul in *Kitab-ı Bahriye* [Book of navigation], late seventeenth century–early eighteenth century. Folio 370b from manuscript W.658. Walters Art Museum, Baltimore. Public domain. https://art.thewalters.org/detail/78190/map-of-the-city-of-constantinople/.

complemented by cypress trees is Seyyid Lokman's 1579 partial map from *Süleymanname*, produced to show the waterway distribution.[76] In this map, with its unique miniature style, the Eyüp district and its surrounding cemeteries outside the city walls are rendered with a level of detail often absent in larger-scale maps, indicating the growing association of cypresses with graves (Figure 19).

By the eighteenth century, bird's-eye views had started to fall out of style, giving way to the dominance of the plan view in cartography. Intriguingly, as the cypress tree solidified its position as the primary indicator of cemeteries, these plan view maps retained the elevation view of the tree to denote burial sites. In the 1740 Gudenus and the 1776 Kauffer maps (the first scientifically scaled map of Istanbul), cemeteries are populated with neatly illustrated cypress tree figures, complemented by descriptive text (Figure 20).[77] The 1740 Gudenus map distinctly presents Üsküdar's cemeteries solely with cypress tree symbols, augmented with the label: "Cipres pilantes sur les Tombeaux des Turcs." Conversely, in the 1764 Reben (Figure 21) and the 1836 Moltke maps, only some of the cemeteries adorned with cypress trees feature accompanying text,

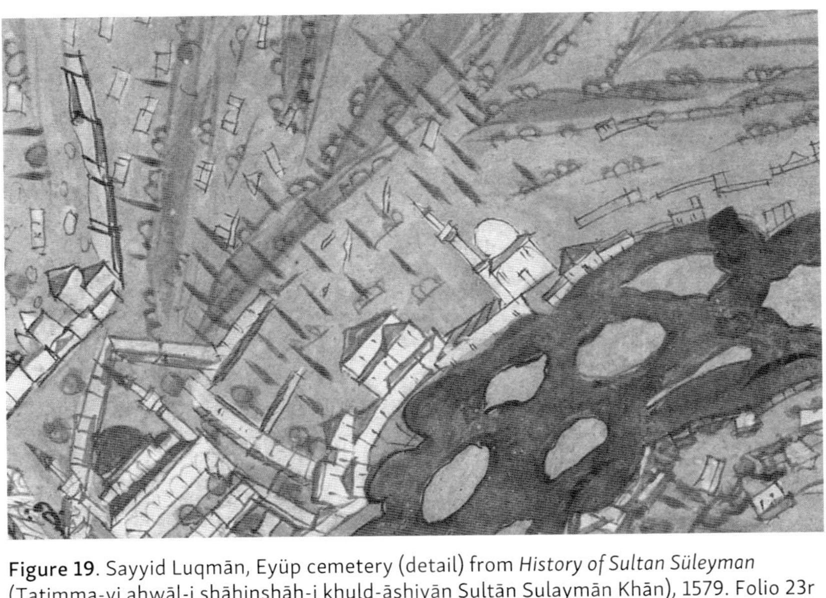

Figure 19. Sayyid Luqmān, Eyüp cemetery (detail) from *History of Sultan Süleyman* (Tatimma-yi aḥwāl-i shāhinshāh-i khuld-āshiyān Sulṭān Sulaymān Khān), 1579. Folio 23r of manuscript T 413. Chester Beatty Library, Dublin. Public Domain. https://viewer.cbl.ie/viewer/image/T_413/45/.

Figure 20. François Kauffer (1751?–1801), Cimetiere Turc (detail) from *Carte de la ville de Constantinople et du canal de la Mer Noire,* 1776. Bibliothèque nationale de France, Département Cartes et Plans, GE AA-3865 (RES). Public domain. https://gallica.bnf.fr/ark:/12148/btv1b72001971.

requiring discernment from viewers to identify other cypress-clad burial grounds.[78] The Pervitich map from 1929 follows a similar pattern, using cypress illustrations to denote burial sites both with and without textual annotations (Figure 22).[79]

The cypress tree ascended to become the unequivocal symbol for cemeteries by the nineteenth century, eliminating the need for any textual supplement. The 1813 Kaminar map, the 1891 Mordtmann map, and the 1919 Raymond map exemplify this kind of muted yet eloquent representation.[80] In two distinct cases, the cypress tree truly shines as an icon—as a form of graphic language rather than a mere visual replica. Unlike most maps, which densely populated the cemeteries with cypress illustrations, the 1919 Raymond map sparingly uses only a few cypress figures to convey the vast expanse of the Eyüp cemetery, thereby elevating the tree to the status of an icon (Figure 23). Similarly, the much earlier 1828 waterways map, with its minimalist design emphasizing only vital details, represents the Karacaahmet cemetery in Üsküdar, at its left bottom, with a few rows of cypress elevations, marking its presence rather than delineating its exact boundaries or topography (Figure 24). Here, the cypress performs purely as a visual sign.

In the 1740 Gudenus map, Christian and Jewish cemeteries are merely indicated by textual labels, devoid of any additional symbols or markers, while Muslim cemeteries are depicted with cypress trees. Similarly, the

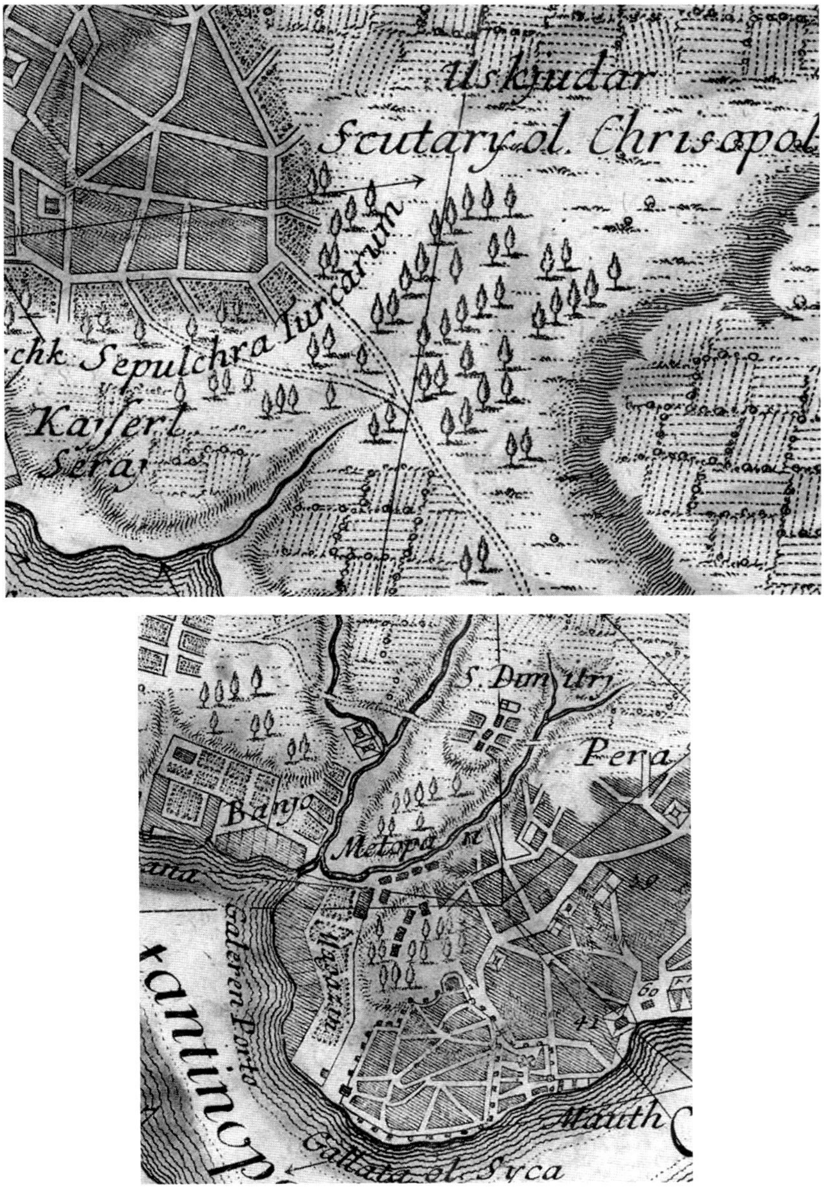

Figure 21. Johann Baptist von Reben, cemetery of Uskudar (detail, *above*) and cemeteries outside Galata (detail, *below*) from *Bosphorus Thracicus, der Kanal des Schwartzen Meers oder die Meer-Enge bey Constantinopel,* 1764. Bibliothèque nationale de France, Département Cartes et Plans, GE C-606. Public domain. https://gallica.bnf.fr/ark:/12148/btv1b530228139/f1.item.

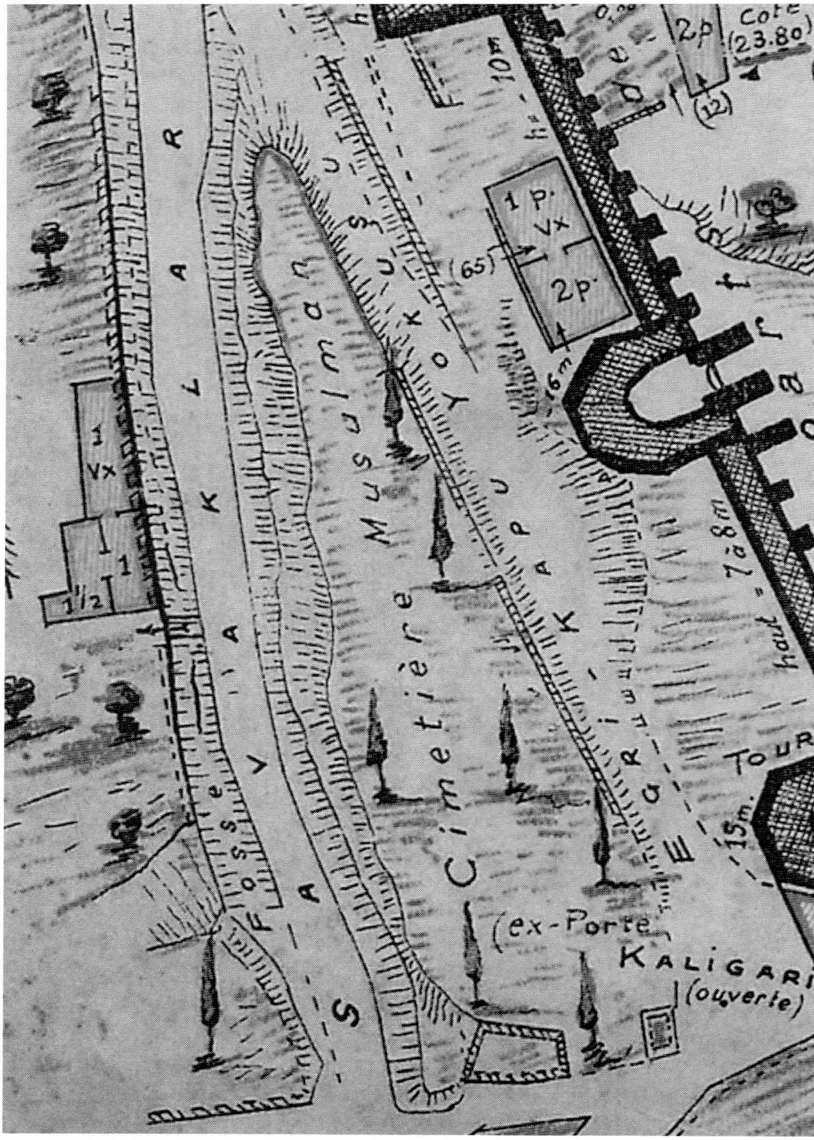

Figure 22. Jacques Pervititch, Cimetiere Musulman (detail) from *29 Aivan-Saray: Les Blakernes, Plan de précision,* 1929. Institut français d'études anatoliennes, KDEAE7E2A1. Digitized in partnership with the Bibliothèque nationale de France, Bibliothèques d'Orient collection. Public domain. https://gallica.bnf.fr/ark:/12148/btv1b10100721v.

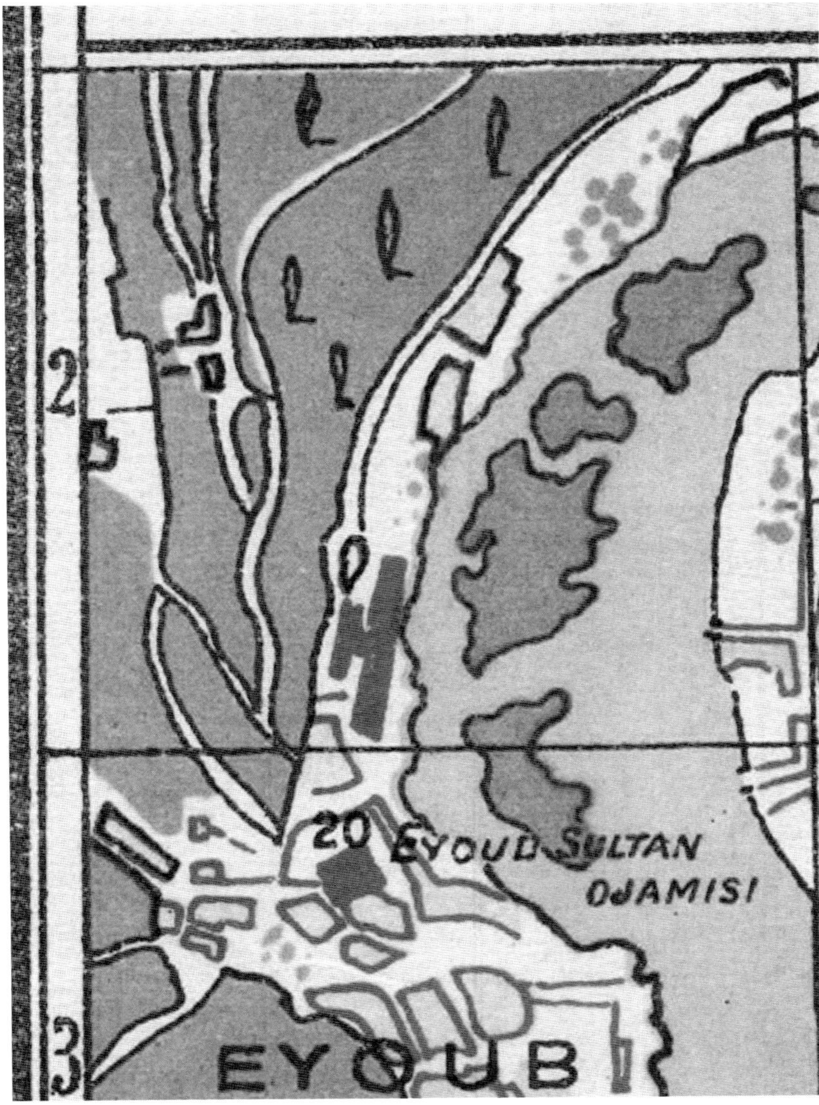

Figure 23. Alexandre M. Raymond, cemetery of Eyüp (detail) from *Plan de Constantinople*, 1919. Communauté des Assomptionnistes de Kadıköy, KD105050A2. Digitized in partnership with the Bibliothèque nationale de France, Bibliothèques d'Orient collection. Public domain. https://gallica.bnf.fr/ark:/12148/btv1b101040456.

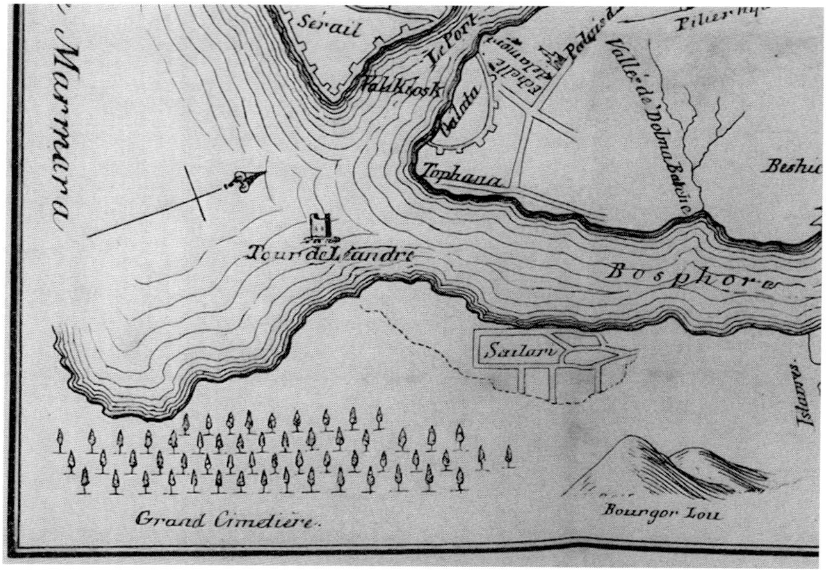

Figure 24. Robert Walsh (1772–1852), cemetery of Uskudar (detail) from *Carte des environs de Constantinople avec les réservoirs et cours d'eau* in *Voyage en Turquie et à Constantinople,* 1828. Wikimedia Commons. Public domain. https://commons.wikimedia.org/wiki/File:Carte_des_environs_de_Constantinople_avec_les_reservoirs_et_cours_d%27eau_-Walsh_Robert-_1828.jpg.

1776 Kauffer map exclusively reserves cypress trees for Muslim burial sites. The Armenian cemetery, by contrast, is signified by an entirely different type of tree, while Greek and Jewish burial sites lack any tree symbols altogether—a representation that may either mirror their real-world appearances during this era or reflect the religious symbolism that the cypress had by then acquired. In the 1918 Necib Bey map, the cypress tree emerges as the main icon selected for Muslim cemeteries, with other symbols, such as Greek cross and dotted line, used for non-Muslim cemeteries (Figure 25). Although we do not know whether there was ever an official regulation governing the use of cypress trees in non-Muslim cemeteries, or this distinction resulted from everyday practice, it seems by this later period, the cypress tree had firmly taken root as the emblem of Muslim cemeteries in the cartographic realm.[81]

Figure 25. Necib Bey, Muslim, Greek, and Jewish cemeteries outside Edirnekapı (detail), from *Composite: 1.1–1.2 Istanbul Eminonu-Fatih, Ayvansaray* from *Necib Bey Maps of Istanbul and Environs,* 1918. David Rumsey Historical Map Collection. Public domain. https://www.davidrumsey.com/luna/servlet/detail/RUMSEY8133098590099407

CONCLUSION

In 1911, architect Le Corbusier poignantly described the fog and clouds over Istanbul, interrelating the three objects of this article: the skyline, the cypress tree, and cemeteries, "They [clouds] come from the depths of the Golden Horn in flocks, they must have gotten stuck in the cypress trees of the cemeteries."[82] Indeed, throughout the Ottoman period, the cypress tree emerged as a potent icon in Istanbul's skyline and in its visual representations, as I suggest here, serving both as an architectural and cartographic marker. I read the cypress as performing an architectural role, *specifically* within Istanbul's unique topography, which allowed for myriad views, silhouettes, and viewing relationships. Through this lens, the cypress made the dead visible within Istanbul's skyline, ensuring they remain part of the living city, while defining Istanbul's spiritual identity as Muslim.

From its earliest representations in panoramic illustrations to its eventual solidification as a sign on two-dimensional maps, the cypress tree's verticality has consistently amplified its prominence. Through its verticality, the cypress tree functioned as a kind of architectural feature for cemeteries, giving them a visibility otherwise impossible in their horizontal layout. Again, it was this verticality that prompted its anthropomorphic function in a cross-cultural symbolic realm, which eventually converged with its architectural perception. As modern architectural theories that frequently invoke the "human body/building" analogy would attest, the strong and perpetual connotation of the cypress tree as human body in the context of arts throughout history supplements the architectural function it took on in Istanbul. In fact, these dimensions worked together, enforcing the eternal presence of the dead—body and soul—onto the city. Varied meanings of the cypress tree in art, literature, local folklore, and practical use converged to shape its particular web of meanings in Istanbul's urban context.

In a metaphorical reading of the local folkloric tradition, each cypress that is immediately planted after internment recovered the physical omission of the body from the material world, replacing its lost verticality. The belief that the cypress tree only flourished and grew if the soul beneath it was blessed suggests that each cypress stood for each faithful "Muslim" dead, whose spiritual presence in turn blessed and protected the city.

Through its reserved association with Muslim cemeteries, the cypress tree contributed to the city's Islamic legitimacy through the ancestral power of the dead. On an individual level, it worked to fulfill the quest for posthumous visibility demanded by societal ambitions (sustaining public identity) and religious fervor (the soul's need for prayers). In a retrospective reading, the cypress tree in Ottoman Istanbul can be seen as an architectural marker in the city's skyline—just as towers, minarets, columns, and living human bodies were—serving as a symbol of eternal life, much as minarets represented piety and columns bore witness to imperial power.

As an afterword, it may be observed that the historical evolution of the cypress tree into the dominant visual sign of cemeteries in Istanbul's skyline reinforced its iconographic role not only in cartography but also in literature. As old *diwan* poetry faded over time and miniature painting left its place to modern fine arts painting, modern Turkish literature extracted the meaning of the cypress tree directly from its material identification with cemeteries—at a time when cypress groves of Istanbul's cemeteries reached their most dense and vast presence, sovereign over the cityscape. Necip Fazıl Kısakürek (1904–1983) embeds the cypress in its urban setting in his "Dear Istanbul": "History has eyes, holes in the ramparts; / Cypress, graceful cypress, curtain for the afterlife . . ."[83] Ahmet Hamdi Tanpınar (1901–1962) placed it strictly in the cemetery: "A pile of soil and a piece of marble, / Written on it your age and name; / On the head side mourning-colored cypresses / Vibrate, as if, with life's sadness."[84] Sabahattin Ali's (1907–1948) cypress is certainly a gravemarker, encouraging death: "A cypress said to me: / Comfort is beneath me."[85] It sometimes retained its association with the human body in classical poetry, however now in the context of death, as Nazım Hikmet (1902–1963) wrote: "I was killed in my bed. Three cypresses. / The cypresses were cut from their roots."[86] The cypress in the cemetery was no longer a marker of eternal life but rather of death, perhaps now seen solely as a source of grief and sorrow—a final, irreversible end. The cypresses, once cut from their roots, would not grow back.[87]

F. İkbal Sezen Polat is an architect and PhD student in architectural history at Middle East Technical University (METU), holding a BA from Mimar Sinan Fine Arts University in Istanbul, Turkey. She is currently a teaching assistant in Gebze Technical University's Department of Architecture. Her research on the cemeteries of Constantinople/Istanbul during the Byzantine and Ottoman periods earned her the Best MA Thesis Award in Social Sciences at METU. She has presented her research at international conferences in Switzerland, the Netherlands, the UK, and the USA, where she has received accolades including the Scott F. Opler Fellowship from the Society of Architectural Historians (SAH) and the Stockton Award from the Association for Gravestone Studies (AGS). She is also part of the DocTalks organizing team, an online platform for PhD students in architectural history and theory.

Notes

The quotation in the title of this article comes from Knut Hamsun and Hans Christian Andersen, *İstanbul'da İki İskandinav Seyyah,* translated by Banu Gürsaler Syvertsen (YKY, 1993), 127.

1. Matthäus Merian, *Constantinopolis-Constantinopolitanae Urbis Effigies ad Vivum Expressa, quam Turcae Stampoldam Vocant A ° MDCXXXV* (Frankfurt, 1638).
2. "Ein aufgemaur der baumgarten mit cypers bäumen" (translated by the author). See 1685 view by Jacob Koppmayr cited in *Göz Alabildiğine İstanbul: Beş Asırdan Manzaralar/Istanbul as Far as the Eye Can See: Views Across Five Centuries,* edited by B. Öztuncay, E. E. Satıcı, and Ş. Çetin (Vehbi Koç Vakfı, 2023), 188.
3. "Ein auf seulen gebauter cybresen wald" (translated by the author). See Johann Baptist Homann, *Stadt Constantinopel* (Nürnberg, 1720).
4. "Ein auf Thürnen gebauter Cypressen garten" (translated by the author). See view by Georg Balthasar Probst (1732–1801) after F. B. Werner (1690–1778) cited in *Göz Alabildiğine İstanbul,* 190.
5. Toklu Dede *hazire*'s history dates back to the Byzantine period. Its graves were attributed to Muslim warriors martyred during the Arab siege of 669. Today, the tombstones and some cypress trees are extant at the site, whereas the thick grove vanished in time. See Stéphanos Yerasimos, *Konstantiniye ve Ayasofya Efsaneleri* (İletişim Yayınları, 1993), 184.
6. This is an episode of urban history that merits further research.
7. Godfrey Goodwin, "Gardens of the Dead in Ottoman Times," *Muqarnas* 5 (1988): 62.
8. Maurice Cerasi, *Osmanlı Kenti: Osmanlı İmparatorluğu'nda 18. Ve 19. Yüzyıllarda Kent Uygarlığı ve Mimarisi* (Yapı Kredi Yayınları, 1999).
9. Reinhold Schiffer, *Oriental Panorama: British Travellers in 19th Century Turkey* (Rodopi, 1999).

10. Marcel Bazin, "La nature à Istanbul," *Géographie et cultures* 62 (2007): 7–26.
11. Godfrey Goodwin, *A History of Ottoman Architecture* (Thames and Hudson, 1997).
12. Comparable uses of cypresses appear in other Ottoman regions, especially in the Balkans and Western Anatolia, though Istanbul provides the most vivid case due to its skyline visibility. Its use in other Ottoman cities merits further research.
13. Hans-Peter Laqueur, "Grabsteine Als Quelle Zur Osmanischen Geschichte-Möglichketien Und Probleme," *Osmanlı Araştırmaları* 3, no. 3 (1982): 21–44, 23.
14. Laqueur; and Joseph de Tournefort, *Tournefort Seyahatnamesi: Birinci Kitap, Ikinci Kitap,* edited by Stefanos Yerasimos (Kitap Yayınevi, 2005), 85.
15. "Comme les cercueils sont sacrés et qu'on déplacerait plutôt une mosquée ou un palais qu'un sépulcre, on est sans cesse obligé d'ouvrir les fosses dans de nouveaux terrains, de telle sorte qu'on ne peut savoir où s'arrêtent les tombeaux. Je me perds quelquefois dans chacun de mes calculs ; je ne vois point ce que deviendra la population vivante de ce pays." Translated by the author from Nicolas Vatin and Stéphane Yerasimos, *Les cimetières dans la ville: Statut, choix et organisation des lieux d'inhumation dans Istanbul intra muros* (Institut français d'études anatoliennes, 2001), 10.
16. The sacredness of cemetery land is established by Islamic law, as recorded in a sixteenth-century *fatwa* by Istanbul's head of religious affairs, Ebussuud. See Vatin and Yerasimos, *Les cimetières dans la ville,* 9.
17. Cemeteries of Pera also became a daily passageway: "Champ des Morts is the promenade of the whole population, Turk, Frank, Greek, and Armenian," in Miss [Julia] Pardoe, *The City of the Sultan, and Domestic Manners of the Turks in 1836* (London, 1837), 138.
18. Antonio Baratta, *Constantinopoli: Effigiata e Descritta* (Turin, 1840), 540.
19. Chateaubriand as cited in Vatin and Yerasimos, *Les cimetières dans la ville,* 10.
20. Currently, in the intra-mural area of the historical peninsula, there are 489 *hazires* of varying sizes. See Vatin and Yerasimos, *Les cimetières dans la ville,* 178. Within the four central and historical districts of the city (Fatih, Beyoğlu, Eyüp, Üsküdar), there exist 706 burial sites, 279 tombs, and 397 stand-alone graves, all of which belong to the Muslim population. See Yunus Ugur, Nicole Kançal-Ferrari, and Alidost Ertugrul, *İstanbul Türbe, Hazire ve Kabirleri: Fatih, Eyüpsultan, Üsküdar, Beyoğlu* (İstanbul Büyükşehir Belediyesi, 2019), 30. Today, within the city's larger municipal borders, there are 564 cemeteries, both Muslim and non-Muslim, covering thirteen million square meters. Historical cemeteries from the nineteenth century or earlier constitute 29 percent of all cemeteries, spanning an area of three million square meters. See Fatıma İkbal Polat, "State of Cemeteries in Istanbul with Regards to Urban Density," in *Aura Istanbul Review Vol.1/2,* edited by İpek İlter (Aura Istanbul, 2019), 134–49.

21. Le Corbusier, *Şark Seyahati: İstanbul 1911*, trans. Alp Tümertekin and Ivan Zaknic (Türkiye İş Bankası Kültür Yayınları, 2009), 88, 126; he also mentions a Turkish saying of the period: "Where there is no house, there is a grave" (translated by the author).
22. Nigel Westbrook, Kenneth Rainsbury Dark, and Rene van Meeuwen, "Constructing Melchior Lorichs's Panorama of Constantinople," *Journal of the Society of Architectural Historians* 69, no. 1 (2010): 62–87.
23. Hamsun and Andersen, *İstanbulda İki İskandinav Seyyah*, 127.
24. Translated by the author from the excerpt on the image (from the British Museum collection, numbered E,6.1-7): "Ilz montent annuellement sur iceulx arbres regardant a vng chascun desdictz arbres, en notant sur quelle sepulture desdictz defunctz son arbre est icelle annee le plushault creu & a surmonte les aultres, pensa. & croyant que l'ame dicelluy qui illec soubz cedict arbre est ensepuely, soit en plushaulte gloire, que les aultres, de qui leurs arbres sont moins accreuz." Pieter Coecke van Aelst, *Les Moeurs et Fachons de Faire de Turcz . . .* (London, 1553), https://www.britishmuseum.org/collection/object/P_E-6-1-7.
25. John Griffiths as cited in Mehmet Karayaman and Buğra İnal, "Seyahatnamelere Göre 19. Yüzyılda Anadolu'da Yaşayan Türklerin Mezar Kültürü," *Uşak Üniversitesi Sosyal Bilimler Dergisi* 10, no. 4 (2017): 675–89. Coecke van Aelst also depicted three individuals in his scene carrying decorated saplings immediately behind the coffin, though it is not clear whether these are cypress saplings (Figure 10).
26. Pardoe, *The City of the Sultan*, 140.
27. The symbolism of the cypress is rather universal and not an Ottoman "invention" per se. The particular focus of this article is its symbolism in Ottoman Istanbul. Notably, the symbolic world of Ottoman *diwan* literature and miniature painting closely follows its predecessor in Persian culture. See Saba Alebrahim Dehkordi, "Studying the Role and Symbolic Meanings of Cypress Tree (Sarv) in Miniatures of 'Tahmasbi Shahnameh,'" *The Scientific Journal of NAZAR Research Center for Art, Architecture & Urbanism* 13, no. 45 (2017): 103–12. Also see Saba Dehkordi, Shahram Taghipoor, and Hamid Rezaei, "A Study on the Significance of Cypress, Plantain, and Vine in Persian Culture, Art, and Literature," *Mediterranean Journal of Social Sciences* 6, no. 6 (2015): 412–16.
28. Jalal Al-Din Rumi, translated by Brad Gooch and Maryam Mortaz, Poetry Foundation, https://www.poetryfoundation.org/poetrymagazine/poems/144612/where-did-the-handsome-beloved-go.
29. Filiz Çağman and Zeren Tanındı as cited in Ceren Pervin Gez, "Türk Mimarisinde Selvi Ağacı Motifi" (Master's thesis, Çanakkale Onsekiz Mart University, 2022), 18. Interestingly, in Byzantine literature, too—alongside being used in burial sites—cypress trees symbolized women's bodies and female beauty. In an anonymous dream interpretation book, the meaning of

the cypress tree was described as a noblewoman. See Vassiliki Kokkori, "Plants as Symbols in Byzantine Oneirocritic Tradition: Imperial Women," *Academia Letters* (August 2021), https://doi.org/10.20935/AL2953. A verse from a Byzantine romantic tale is another instance: "in her youthful vigor she was tall as a young cypress." See Ingela Nilsson, "Words, Water, and Power: Literary Fountains and Metaphors of Patronage in Eleventh- and Twelfth-Century Byzantium," in *Fountains and Water Culture in Byzantium,* edited by B. Shilling and P. Stephenson (Cambridge University Press, 2016), 265–80, 282.

30. Afterward Apollo said to him: "You shall be mourned by me, shall mourn for others, and your place shall always be where others grieve." Ovid, *Metamorphoses* 10 as cited in Virginia L. Campbell, "Stopping to Smell the Roses: Garden Tombs in Roman Italy," *Arctos: Acta Philologica Fennica* 42 (2008): 31–43, 34. For other accounts of the myth, see Robin Hard, *The Routledge Handbook of Greek Mythology,* 8th ed. (Routledge, 2019).
31. Moreover, another instance from Byzantine art visually converges human body and cypress tree. In the eleventh-century Byzantine chronicle of John Skylitzes, an illustration portraying a cypress tree with a human inside belongs to this passage: "Depressed and distressed though she was, in her sleep she saw a huge tree like a cypress, standing in her atrium . . . her son, Basil, was seated at the top of it." See John Skylitzes and John Wortley, *John Skylitzes: A Synopsis of Byzantine History, 811–1057: Translation and Notes* (Cambridge University Press, 2010), 122. For the image, see Image 177 in John Skylitzes, *History of Byzantium (Palermo, Italy, 1100 to 1299),* https://www.loc.gov/item/2021667859/.
32. Yusuf Çetin and Bahar Yayık, "Tasavvuf Düşüncesinde Servi Ağacı Ve Türk-İslam Sanatındaki Yansımaları," *Türk Kültürü ve Hacı Bektaş Veli Araştırma Dergisi* 100 (December 2021): 485–514, 496.
33. Çetin and Yayık, 497. As mentioned earlier, Julia Pardoe described the bending at the top of the cypress tree as a bad omen. The fact that the same form is interpreted differently in folklore and Sufi culture is not unusual.
34. "Geldikce berg-i sebz ile dogruluban şehâ / Bu tekyegâh-ı ʿâleme dervîşvâr serv" (K11–23), [O Shah, each time it rises upright with its green leaves / The cypress stands like a dervish in this lodge of the world.] (translated by the author), as cited in Mutlu Melis Özgeriş, Faris Karahan, and Mustafa Özgeriş, "Servi Ağacının Türk Kültürü ve Peyzajında Kazandığı Anlamların Hayâlî'nin 'Serv' Redifli Kasidesindeki Yansımaları," *Anemon Muş Alparslan Üniversitesi Sosyal Bilimler Dergisi* 10, no. 1 (2022): 273–87, 272, 273.
35. For the "Tree of Life" in global cultural history, see Roger Cook, *The Tree of Life* (Thames and Hudson, 1974). For the "Tree of Life" cult in Turkish culture, see Seher Arslan, "Türk Kültüründe Ağaç Kültü ve Hayat Ağacı," *Uluslararası Sosyal ve Eğitim Bilimleri Dergisi* 1, no. 1 (2014): 59–71.
36. According to Michel Ragon, because of its strength, the cypress was naturally chosen as the symbol of immortality in many cultures. Chaldeans, Syrians,

and Assyrians regarded it sacred. See Michel Ragon, *The Space of Death: A Study of Funerary Architecture, Decoration, and Urbanism,* translated by Alan Sheridan (University of Virginia Press, 1983). Also see Cynthia Wagner Weick, Naela Aamir, and Jayme Reichart, "The Ethnobotanical Evolution of the Mediterranean Cypress (Cupressus sempervirens)," *Econ Bot* 77 (2023): 203–21, 207.

37. *Ab-ı hayat* is the legendary water believed to bring immortality to those who drink it. See Ahmet Yaşar Ocak, "Âb-ı Hayât," *TDV İslâm Ansiklopedisi,* 1988, https://islamansiklopedisi.org.tr/ab-i-hayat#1-tasavvuf.
38. Çetin and Yayık, "Tasavvuf Düşüncesinde Servi Ağacı."
39. Recep Kankal, "Türk Kültüründe Servi Ağacı/Cypress Tree in Turkish Culture," *YEE Culture Magazine of Turkey* 11 (2016): 51.
40. Ömer Delikgöz and Fulya Alıç, "Osmanlı İstanbul'unda Bulunan Bazı Müslim ve Gayrimüslim Mezarlıklarındaki Kimi Semboller," *Hacettepe Üniversitesi Türkiyat Araştırmaları Dergisi* 13 (2010): 113–131, 116. In an artistic context where Islamic tradition prohibited the visual depiction of humans, botanical representations often emerged as an innovative solution. On Islamic visual arts under the influence of the prohibition of the human image, see Oleg Grabar, "Islamic Attitudes Towards Art," in *The Formation of Islamic Art* (Yale University Press, 1973), 75–104.
41. Delikgöz and Alıç, 116.
42. Cerasi, *Osmanlı Kenti,* 201. Ancient Israelites rejected the use of flowers or plants for funerals and graves, differing from other religions. See Amots Dafni et al., "Ritual Plants of Muslim Graveyards in Northern Israel," *Journal of Ethnobiology Ethnomedicine* 2, no. 38 (2006): 2. Greek and Armenian cemeteries, on the other hand, also contained cypress trees among other vegetation, though never as dominant as in Muslim cemeteries.
43. Delikgöz and Alıç, "Osmanlı İstanbul'unda Bulunan Bazı Müslim ve Gayrimüslim Mezarlıklarındaki Kimi Semboller," 115.
44. The date 6411 on the inscription means CE 903. See Cyril Mango, "The Funeral Tree: A Newly-Discovered Byzantine Inscription from Istanbul," *Archaeology* 3, no. 3 (1950): 141.
45. Mango, 140.
46. For Silivrikapı Hypogeum, see Johannes Georg Deckers and Ümit Serdaroğlu, "Das Hypogäum Beim Silivri-Kapi in Istanbul," in *Akten Des XII. Internationalen Kongresses Für Christliche Archäologie Bonn, September 22–28, 1991, Vols. 1–2* (Aschendorff, 1995), 674–681; Ivan Foletti, "Of Holes and a Holy Man: New Discoveries in the Silivri-Kapı Mausoleum in Istanbul," *Kunstchronik* 66, no. 4 (2013): 178–82; and Mehmet İ. Tunay, "Byzantine Archaeological Findings in Istanbul During the Last Decade," in *Byzantine Constantinople: Monuments, Topography and Everyday Life,* edited by N. Necipoğlu (Brill, 2001), 217–31.
47. Theod. Metoch., Encom. Nic. 11, cited in Veronica Della Dora, *Landscape, Nature, and the Sacred in Byzantium* (Cambridge University Press, 2016), 111, 116.

48. In the amalgamation of the Ottoman culture, made of Old Turkic, Persian, Islamic, Greco-Roman, and Byzantine cultures, any symbolism is multi-sourced. In the elite forms of art and literature—namely *diwan* poetry and miniature painting—that are imported from Persian traditions, the cypress predominantly retained its Persian connotations, whereas Istanbul's (and Anatolia's) local folklore favored narratives, beliefs, and practices that were more regionally anchored, that is of Mesopotamian and Greco-Roman respectively. This duality—of foreign import and local adaptation—showcases the multifaceted significance of the cypresses in the Ottoman cultural milieu.
49. Ragon, *The Space of Death*, 114.
50. In Roman belief, death polluted the house and the family. "According to Servius, the marking of the death-house was intended as a warning of possible pollution," see Hugh Lindsay, "Death-Pollution and Funerals in the City of Rome," in *Death and Disease in The Ancient City*, edited by V. M. Hope and E. Marshall (Routledge, 2000), 155.
51. Catherine Connors, "Seeing Cypresses in Virgil," *The Classical Journal* 88, no. 1 (1992): 1–17, 1.
52. Mango, "The Funeral Tree," 140; Dafni et al., "Ritual Plants of Muslim Graveyards," 5.
53. Roman scholar Varro recorded that the cypress tree was used to cover the strong smell coming from the body in combustion. See M. Herrera Valenciano, "Uso del ciprés como árbol funerario en Roma Antigua," *Káñina* 41, no. 2 (2017): 67–85, 69.
54. Murat Dursun Tosun, "Servi-Selvi Ağacının Hikâyesi," https://muratdursuntosun.wordpress.com/2016/05/31/servi-selvi-agacinin-hikayesi/. Also see Kankal, "Türk Kültüründe Servi Ağacı/Cypress Tree in Turkish Culture," 57.
55. Nina Ergin, "The Fragrance of the Divine: Ottoman Incense Burners and Their Context," *Art Bulletin* 96, no. 1 (2014): 70–97, 78.
56. Hamsun and Andersen, *İstanbul'da İki İskandinav Seyyah*, 38.
57. Spiro Kostof, *The City Shaped: Urban Patterns and Meanings Through History* (Little, Brown, 1991) as cited in Pelin Yoncacı Arslan, "Christianizing the Skyline: The Appropriation of the Pagan Honorary Column in Early Constantinople" (PhD diss., University of California, Los Angeles, 2015), 254, 255.
58. Some of the examples include: "Gülşen münevver oldı serâser Medine-vâr / Kumrular anda mukrî olurlar menâr serv" (Necâtî D., K. 21, b. 9, s. 102), [The rose garden was filled with light like Medina / The cypress tree became a minaret, the doves read the Quran on it] (translated by the author), as cited in Gülümser Özerden, "Divan Şiirinde Servi (15. Ve 16. Yüzyıllar)" (Master's thesis, Çukurova University, 2015), 3. "Âşıklarun namâzın kılmagıçün salâya / Her serv-i ser-firâzun kaddi minârelerdür" (Behiştî D., G. 99, b. 3, s. 282), [To call (sala) for performing the lovers' prayer / The tall cypresses, each with their heads up, are minarets] (translated by the author) as cited in Özerden, 84.

59. "Mukri'dür anda bülbül-i şeydâ menâr serv (Hayali, K11–9)" (translated by the author), as cited in Özgeriş, Karahan, and Özgeriş, "Servi Ağacının Türk Kültürü ve Peyzajında Kazandığı Anlamlar," 272, 273.
60. "Temâşâ eylesen her bir minâre / Dönüpdür serv-kâmet bir nigâra (Mesîhî D., Şehrengiz, b. 62, s. 94)" (translated by the author), as cited in Özerden, *Divan Şiirinde Servi,* 84.
61. The *türbe,* or monumental mausoleum, was traditionally built for emperors, rulers, and religious figures. During the Ottoman period, with the rise of the elite and the *wakf* (charitable foundation) system, it became common for elite members to build tombs near their endowed buildings and have their families buried in the adjoining graveyard (*hazire*). While intramural burial was banned for common people, this system allowed a privileged few to be interred within the city, linking the visibility of death to urban prosperity. For Istanbul's *türbes*, see Halil İbrahim Düzenli, "The Tombs of Istanbul," *A History of Istanbul,* https://istanbultarihi.ist/710-the-tombs-of-istanbul.
62. For discussions about tomb building in Islamic history see Leor Halevi, "The Politics of Burial and Tomb Construction," in *Muhammad's Grave: Death Rites and the Making of Islamic Society,* 165 (Columbia University Press, 2007). Even tombstones have been controversial in some fundamentalist approaches, see Halevi, "Traditionist Opposition to Tombstones," in *Muhammed's Grave,* 32–38. In the seventeenth-century Istanbul, the extremist religious movement of "*Kadızadelis*" protested against building tombs. Consequently, for a while, open-grill dome tombs were opted. See Mustafa Çağhan Keskin, "'Do Not Build a Dome and Monuments on Me': Uncovered Tomb Taste in Ottoman Architecture (1661–1763)," *Osmanlı Araştırmaları: The Journal of Ottoman Studies* 55 (2020): 51–98.
63. Gülru Necipoğlu, "Dynastic Imprints on the Cityscape," in *İslâm Dünyasında Mezarlıklar ve Defin Gelenekleri* (Türk Tarih Kurumu, 1996), 123–34.
64. Edhem Eldem, *Death in Istanbul: Death and Its Rituals in Ottoman-Islamic Culture* (Ottoman Bank Archives and Research Centre, 2005), 25; and Maurice Cerasi, *Divanyolu* (Kitap Yayınevi, 2006), 66–72, 142.
65. About praying for the dead and visitation of graves in Islam, see Werner Diem and Schöller Marco, *The Living and the Dead in Islam. Studies in Arabic Epitaphs: Epitaphs as Texts* (Harrassowitz Verlag, 2004).
66. "They build cemeteries by the roadside like the ancient Romans." See Pardoe, *The City of the Sultan,* 138. Roman cemeteries "were beyond the boundaries, but very close to the urban center, and also clustered around the major roads leaving the city." Also, their motivation was similar to that of the Ottomans: "It meant that the tombs of the dead were regularly and clearly visible to large numbers of people, helping to perpetuate their memory. . . . It also meant that they were easily accessible for living relatives to visit and make offerings." See Penelope J. Goodman, *The Roman City and Its Periphery: From Rome to Gaul* (Routledge, 2007), 150.

67. Pardoe, *The City of the Sultan*, 138, 147.
68. Pardoe, 149.
69. Antonio Baratta contemplates on the topic: "Cypresses are abundant in the area occupied by the Turks, while the most joyful and kind plants are found in the regions of the Armenians and Greeks, and so on. The cemeteries of the Jews are the most squalid of all, with few or no trees and no decorative or grand features. We don't know whether this is due to a reason unknown to us, a hidden religious precept, their heightened political fear in Turkey, or the thrift—a thrift which I now often criticize in ourselves" (translated by the author); Baratta, *Costantinopoli: Effigiata e Descritta*, 532.
70. Çiğdem Kafesçioğlu, "The Ottoman Capital in the Making" (PhD diss., Harvard University, 1996), 375.
71. For a concise review of foreign maps of Istanbul, see Ayşe Yetişkin Kubilay, "Maps of Istanbul in Western Sources," History of Istanbul, https://istanbul tarihi.ist/397-maps-of-istanbul-in-western-sources. For an introduction to Ottoman-produced maps of Istanbul, see İrfan Dağdelen, "Istanbul in Ottoman Maps," History of Istanbul, https://istanbultarihi.ist/398-istanbul -in-ottoman-maps.
72. Finding any representation of a cemetery in these fifteenth-century maps is highly significant, showing Istanbul's uniqueness in terms of burial topography. In this century, most European cities did not have cemeteries but crowded burials in the limited grounds of churchyards.
73. Sixteenth and seventeenth-century Istanbul maps that depict cemeteries only with tombstones include: Salomon Schweigger, "Eigentlicher Ubriss der Stadt Constantinopel," in *Ein newe Reiss Beschreibung auss Teutschland nach Constantinopel und Jerusalem* (Nürnberg, 1608), 102; and a seventeenth-century anonymous Ottoman map published by Cahit Kayra in 1990. See Funda Baş Bütüner, "Urban Fissure: Reconceptualization of the Land Walls within the Urban Milieu of Istanbul" (PhD diss., Middle East Technical University, 2010), 71; and Jaspar Isaac, "La Ville de Constantinople" (Paris, circa 1620).
74. Although based on the 1526 original, the Walters copy of *Kitab-ı Bahriye* is dated to the late seventeenth century, one possible date being 1682. See Paul Hepworth, "Production and Date of the Walters' 'Kitab-i Bahriye,'" *Journal of the Walters Art Museum* 63 (January 2005): 73–80.
75. In this copy and in a Paris copy, only those who are familiar with Pera's burial grounds can identify them on the map. They portray them as dense cypress groves, interrupting the urban milieu. Also in the Paris copy, one can discern the early stage of Eyüp cemetery, marked distinctly by a row of five cypress trees. About the Paris copy (Suppl. Turc 956, fol. 434v. at Bibliothèque Nationale de France) see Çiğdem Kafesçioğlu, "Viewing, Walking, Mapping Istanbul, ca. 1580," *Mitteilungen Des Kunsthistorischen Institutes in Florenz* 56 (2014): 17–36, 27.

76. Kafesçioğlu, 21.
77. Kubilay, "Maps of Istanbul in Western Sources." François Kauffer's 1776 and 1786 maps remain the most reliable source of information for the burial topography of eighteenth-century Istanbul. Moreover, thanks to the close scale of the 1786 version, unprecedented information on cemeteries is available, including Christian and Jewish cemeteries and the concentrated areas of tombstones.
78. Helmuth van Moltke's 1836 map was the subsequent scientifically scaled map of Istanbul after Kauffer's, prepared by the order of Mahmud II. See Murat Gül and Richard Lamb, "Mapping, Regularizing, and Modernizing Ottoman Istanbul: Aspects of the Genesis of the 1839 Development Policy," *Urban History* 31, no. 3 (2004): 420–36.
79. This critically acclaimed close-scaled map was crafted by Pervititch in 1929 specifically for a fire insurance company. See Jacques Pervititch, *Istanbul in the Insurance Maps of Jacques Pervititch* (Tarih Vakfı/Aksa Oyak Yayınları, 2000).
80. Although Konstantin Kaminar's 1813 watercolor, an Ottoman-made map in the beginning of nineteenth century, follows the pre-Kauffer style, it shows cemeteries in a very conspicuous manner by using cypress trees. See Dağdelen, "Istanbul in Ottoman Maps."
81. The discrepancies among sources such as travel accounts, photographs, and maps regarding the vegetation differences between Muslim and non-Muslim cemeteries in Istanbul merit a separate study. Historical photographs depict certain non-Muslim cemeteries, such as the Hasköy Jewish Cemetery or the Taksim Surp Agop Armenian Cemetery, as largely devoid of vegetation. By contrast, today non-Muslim cemeteries—including Bağlarbaşı Greek Cemetery, Ortaköy Greek Cemetery, Balıklı Armenian Cemetery, and Feriköy Catholic Cemetery, among others—contain cypress trees alongside other species. Whether this discrepancy reflects historical transformation or another factor remains to be investigated. It is nevertheless noteworthy that late Ottoman maps consistently depict only Muslim cemeteries with the cypress symbol, with no exceptions I have observed.
82. Le Corbusier, *Şark Seyahati*, 108.
83. Mehlika Afra Cebeci, "İstanbul Peyzaj Kültüründe Servi Ağacının Yeri" (Master's thesis, İstanbul Bilgi University, 2019), 37. For other references to the cypress tree in modern Turkish poetry, see Cebeci, 30–38.
84. Cebeci, 36.
85. Cebeci, 38.
86. Cebeci, 37.
87. In the late nineteenth and early twentieth centuries, cypresses were literally removed from cemeteries that were being demolished. There are a number of documents in the Ottoman archives concerning cypress trees in cemeteries (a subject I examine more fully in my ongoing doctoral research); however, they fall outside the scope of this article. Here, I will suffice with pointing to a 1902

document from the Ottoman State Archives that ordered the cutting and sale of cemetery cypresses. See Ottoman State Archives, Yıldız Palace Perakende Evrakı (Y..PRK.ZB..)-, no. 32/15, 14 Zilkade 1319, February 22, 1902. To create new urban quarters, public roads, or parks, several major historical cemeteries were destroyed. For the destruction of the Pera cemeteries in the nineteenth century, see Nahide Işık Demirakın, "Expropriation as a Modernizing Tool in the Nineteenth-Century Ottoman Empire," *International Journal of Turkish Studies* 18, no. 1/2 (2012): 1–15. For the destruction of the Eğrikapı cemeteries in the late twentieth century, see Hans-Peter Laqueur, *Hüve'l-Baki: İstanbul'da Osmanlı Mezarlıkları ve Mezar Taşları* (Tarih Vakfı Yurt Yayınları, 1993), 27.

Book Reviews

John H. Jameson, Sherene Baugher, and Richard Veit, eds. *Monuments and Memory: Archaeological Perspectives on Commemoration.*

University Press of Florida, 2025.
xii + 303 pp. ISBN 978-0-8130-7923-3.

The last decade has witnessed a veritable glut in scholarship addressing the challenges and controversies associated with monuments and memorialization in the United States. The public memory of the Civil War, and more particularly monuments associated with the former Confederacy, has received the lion's share of attention. Rightly so, given the controversies attached to such monuments, but this has meant that commemorative objects and spaces associated with other historical conflicts, social movements, and significant people have remained underrepresented within the extant literature. As such, *Monuments and Memory: Archaeological Perspectives on Commemoration*, a collection of essays edited by John H. Jameson, Sherene Baugher, and Richard Veit, is a refreshingly welcome addition to this area of study. With sixteen chapters arranged chronologically by historical event and "the heritage narrative," *Monuments and Memory* addresses important issues in both historical and contemporary memorialization practices such as "silenced history" as well as "the social and cultural factors that influence the erection of monuments" (12).

As noted by the volume's editors, a common theme uniting all the essays is that "the monuments represent an archaeology of conflict" (12). The notion of conflict here can be understood in a couple of different ways. The monuments and memorial spaces addressed in these chapters were created to commemorate historical events involving conflict, war being the most common. A second way to interpret the theme of conflict is how, especially in the twenty-first century, the monuments themselves have generated conflicts over issues of historical interpretation and matters concerning whose voices and experiences are recognized and whose remain silenced. Inspired by "the recent re-eruption of fundamental unresolved inequities at the core of American society" (277), Jameson, Baugher, and Veit state, "In a post-George Floyd era, monuments can make previously silenced voices heard; they can be empowering by affirming the identity and restoring the dignity of marginalized groups" (15).

Thus, even as society reckons with the darker aspects of the American past and the monuments erected as testaments to white supremacy and systemic racism, Americans today have the opportunity to approach memorialization projects and sites of memory in new ways that celebrate the achievements of those who, historically, have been ignored.

While several chapters address monuments as traditionally conceived—sculptural or architectural objects placed on the landscape and dedicated to an individual, group, or specific event—many of the chapters in *Monuments and Memory* challenge our very notion of what constitutes a monument. For example, Kerri Barile Tambs's chapter on Fredericksburg, Virginia's slave auction block explores how a 2.5 foot tall column of sandstone, "an object that enslaved individuals purportedly stood on to be sold as chattel" (40), stood as a historical monument "to the [racial] discord that has existed [in Fredericksburg] for well over a century" (51). In this instance, the block was not placed after-the-fact, as is generally the case with commemorative objects, but rather the artifact itself, in its perpetual survival on the changing urban landscape, was transformed over time *into* a monument that recalled the city's historical slave trade. Mark Cassello's engaging chapter on the town of Pullman in Chicago considers how this model factory town was declared a national monument by President Barack Obama. By examining the establishment of the Pullman National Monument and its fraught relationship with the A. Philip Randolph Museum (dedicated to the history of the African American Pullman Porters), Cassello explores "the place and cultural factors that have influenced which narratives are told in Pullman" and which remain absent (145).

Suzanne Spencer-Wood's chapter offers an important counterpoint to the other fifteen chapters in this volume, as it specifically addresses the dearth of monuments to women and people of color on the American commemorative landscape. She provides important quantitative data on the actual number of monuments to women and minorities to support her contention that "more statues of minorities and women are needed in the national and state capitals to remind legislators to serve the interests of the diversity of people who elected them and stop taking away voting rights and women's right to bodily autonomy" (165). Spencer-Wood concludes her chapter with her recommendations for the erection of monuments to four important women whose historical contributions have remained ignored.

Even as the rest of the chapters fall into the category of addressing war-related monuments, with five dealing specifically with sites and structures related to the Civil War, there are important additions to the preexisting scholarship on war memorialization efforts. Timo Ylimaunu and Paul R. Mullins offer a fascinating comparative study of monuments to defeat in their examination of the Finnish and American civil wars—

while the vanquished in Finland's civil war were ultimately able to erect public memorials to the dead, the purpose and symbolism of those monuments contrast sharply with the defiant nature of Confederate monuments in the United States. Levi Fox's important chapter on Korean War memorials is arguably the first standalone study on this subject and he considers how the "memory boom" of the 1980s to the early twenty-first century contributed to fashioning the public's perception of Korea as "the Forgotten War" despite the numerous local and state monuments dedicated to both the living and the dead who fought in this conflict. With her chapter concerning the life cycle of memorials at Fort Monmouth, New Jersey, a military installation that closed in 2011, Melissa Ziobro asks important questions concerning the "birth" and "death" of memorials, along with what "long-term responsibilities do we have to individuals memorialized?" (237).

The essays gathered in *Monuments and Memory* provide an important contribution to the fields of public history, memory studies, and material culture. Even as several of the chapters explore the already well-trod ground of Civil War memorialization, they nevertheless provide novel approaches to reframing how scholars and communities engage with or challenge the historical narratives they propound. *Monuments and Memory* will be useful to educators and students as well as to scholars, as many of the chapters break new ground on subjects hitherto largely unexplored and will undoubtedly be used as launch points for further studies.

Joy M. Giguere
Associate Professor of History
Penn State York

Adam Rosenblatt. ***Cemetery Citizens: Reclaiming the Past and Working for Justice in American Burial Grounds.***

Stanford University Press, 2024.
272 pp. ISBN 978-1-5036-3911-9.

Adam Rosenblatt, associate professor of practice at Duke University, describes his book as "activist anthropology" (as noted in his LinkedIn promotion and on the back cover). The term proves fitting as the narrative unfolds and Rosenblatt embeds himself in the world of what he calls "Cemetery Citizens."

Who are Cemetery Citizens? According to Rosenblatt, they are "people who found themselves in a place where the dead seemed abandoned—maybe not by the people who loved them, but by the surrounding world. They asked questions and got curious . . . soon their questions became projects" (2). As someone who also identifies as a Cemetery Citizen, I found this work deeply resonant and thought-provoking.

The book situates itself within the historiography of cemetery studies, drawing on anthropology, history, and activism within marginalized places. Rosenblatt focuses on three African American cemeteries—Geer Cemetery in Durham, NC; East End

Cemetery in Richmond, VA; and Mount Moriah Cemetery in Philadelphia, PA. He frames the work at these sites not as "restoration" but as "revision," a term that reflects both acknowledgment of past neglect and an openness to imagining new futures. In one of his poetic narratives, the author writes:

> Revision is not fixing,
> or setting names and meanings in stone.
> Revision is broken world thinking:
> Here is this boat, it's smashed.
> What do we make out of it? Is there a future for it? . . .
> Here is the past: it's both terrible
> and utterly ours. We own it . . . .
> (123–124)

Rosenblatt offers the notion that cemetery preservation in marginalized cemeteries is a chance to revise history. Not in a negative, revisionistic history sort of way, but as an honest reckoning of legacies of violence, erasure, and exclusion. In this revision, cemeteries become public gathering places where volunteers of all races honor the dead together. Where silence once reigned, celebration now emerges.

The title, *Cemetery Citizens: Reclaiming the Past and Working for Justice in American Burial Grounds*, reflects the book's scope. It asks and answers essential questions: Who is doing the work? What are they doing? When are they doing it, and when were these cemeteries founded? Where are these cemeteries, and what is their spatial significance? And most importantly—why? Why are people compelled to do this work?

Rosenblatt's approach is infused with emotion. His conversations with Cemetery Citizens, along with sketches and interviews presented in poetic form, bring the personal and affective dimensions of activism to the foreground. The stylistic choice of using a poetry format for interviews underscores how participants feel about their work, as well as how Rosenblatt himself processes these experiences. This work is very much about feelings, for better or worse, especially for those who choose to preserve, protect, and revise cemeteries.

With his focus on African American cemeteries, Rosenblatt addresses the concept of "death privilege"—the inequities in whose graves are preserved and respected—and invites readers to confront difficult questions of memory, justice, and responsibility, and what privilege means in these settings. As a volunteer in a predominantly white burial ground that once faced similar neglect, I was struck by the parallels to Rosenblatt's case studies. His exploration of meaning-making—asking what restoration creates for Cemetery Citizens, for the cemeteries, and for the dead (129)—is compelling, especially as the answers differ between sites and individuals.

At the same time, I wished for deeper engagement with theoretical frameworks such as Maurice Halbwachs's collective memory or Henri Lefebvre's spatial theory, which could have enriched the analysis of how Cemetery Citizens negotiate the past through physical space. Similarly, Rosenblatt briefly acknowledges silences—"So much loss is permanent in these cemeteries, grave markers are gone, records are lost, archives are fragmentary" (34–35)—but further discussion could tie these archival silences more explicitly to the structural causes of erasure in marginalized communities surrounding these cemeteries. But that would mean a much larger book. I am hoping for a second volume.

One major question lingers, perhaps deliberately unanswered: Why devote scarce resources to cemetery work when people are facing hunger, illness, and poverty? The book suggests, but does not fully resolve, how care for the dead intersects with care for the living. Written during the COVID-19 pandemic, the book intertwines reflections on burial activism with the unfolding global crisis. In doing so, it becomes not only a contribution to cemetery scholarship but also a record of contemporary history and activism. In today's climate, where calls for engaged scholarship grow louder, Rosenblatt's work is both timely and necessary.

Cemetery Citizens is a vital contribution to the study of cemeteries and public memory. It speaks to scholars, practitioners, and community members alike, offering inspiration as well as a challenge: to view cemeteries not as silent ruins but as living sites of memory, justice, and repair. Most of all, Rosenblatt leaves Cemetery Citizens with a haunting and necessary question: Why do you do the work that you do?

Jennifer Shaffer Merry
Archivist and Historian
Arizona Historical Society

Joy M. Giguere. *Pleasure Grounds of Death: The Rural Cemetery in Nineteenth-Century America.*

University of Michigan Press, 2024. xiii + 275 pp. ISBN 9780472076895 (hardcover), 9780472056897 (paperback).

Giguere opens with Dell Upton's "reform cemeteries" —their chartering as corporations perhaps more innovative than their geometric "neoclassical grid" (44). The first was New Haven's Grove Street Cemetery in 1796. Paris had experienced similar problems with disease and overcrowding, and in 1804, the Republic assumed civil control over burial and opened Père Lachaise, rejecting French geometric horticultural traditions for a picturesque English country park design. Though eventually overrun with family tombs and enlarged by rectilinear accretions it became the prototype for the North American "rural cemetery" though not immediately taken up. Giguere highlights the debates inspired by public health crises in the 1820s that gave rise to reform cemeteries in New York (the 1823 City Burying Ground, now Bryant Park, solely for the poor), and Philadelphia where business associations established private cemeteries that *excluded* the poor. In Boston, Père Lachaise became the inspiration for the prototypical Mount Auburn of 1831, an initiative of the Massachusetts Horticultural Society.

This is very much a book on the United States as the author seldom ventures beyond its borders apart from the necessary allusions to Père Lachaise. What about the non-denominational cemetery akin to Grove Street laid out beyond the walls of Montreal in 1799 (Brian Young, *Respectable Burial,* 6)? Whether or not inspired by New Haven, there were old world precedents for both, notably London's seventeenth-century non-Conformist ground, Bunhill Fields. James Stevens Curl and Thomas Kselman explore cultural currents in England and France that presaged the rural or garden cemetery.

Giguere does cite early Canadian novelist T. C. Haliburton's itinerant Yankee clockmaker, astutely observing (1841) that rural cemeteries were grand places for courtship as "it's so romantic" that the landscape "will put all the dead in creation out of your head a'most" (87–88). This was one reason some Catholic commentators opposed the model. Giguere's analysis is attentive to race, somewhat less so to religious differences. She acknowledges that some Catholic dioceses were receptive and some not and references Allan Amanik's recent work on Jewish rural cemeteries, both insisting on denominational exclusivity. Did some Protestant denominations establish exclusive burial grounds, and incorporate or reject rural cemetery ideals? Julie Rugg has reminded us that in England parish churchyards continued to proliferate alongside garden cemeteries, with inevitable cultural cross-fertilization. Influence on American country cemeteries has been little studied.

Giguere tends to blur dedication and consecration, or perhaps her sources do. In his consecration address at Mount Auburn, Joseph Story (Supreme Court justice and Mount Auburn Association president) emphasized protection in law: the legislative authority to perpetually dedicate burial grounds. Denominational consecration became an issue in Canada and Bermuda, notably in the 1870s when some Anglican parishes denied burial in family plots to non-Anglicans, and the Guibord case in Quebec prompted adjudication on the right of the Catholic Church to refuse burial in religiously consecrated ground. France experienced renewed disputation between civil and religious authorities over control of burial and even the placement of First World War memorials, and in Britain, religious objections obstructed cremation.

This thoughtful volume follows publication of two others similarly claiming national scope. Though jacket accolades for *Grave Landscapes: The Nineteenth-Century Rural Cemetery Movement* by the late James Cothran and Erica Danylchak (University of South Carolina Press, 2018) claim it contains "quite literally everything you ever wanted to know about the rural cemetery movement," it focuses on its landscape influence and histories of prominent cemeteries but takes diffusion of the model from the Northeast largely for granted. Giguere has noted a common presumption that urban southerners simply adopted northern models. She argues that postbellum reinvention as shrines to the Confederate dead obscured how Southern rural cemeteries strove to inscribe southern cities into the American cultural and political narrative and combat the long-standing equation of American culture with New England. Intentions differed regionally, but also from cemetery to cemetery, and the model proved adaptable to cultures, landscapes, and climates.

Jeffrey Smith's *The Rural Cemetery Movement: Places of Paradox in Nineteenth-Century America* (Lexington Books, 2017) is organized around the paradoxes: "'rural' yet urban, sacred yet secular, . . . for the dead but used regularly by the living, natured yet manicured" (xi). He is particularly interested in them as businesses with burials subsidizing functions serving the living. He draws usefully upon minute books, published regulations and guidebooks, and after 1889 the *Proceedings* of the Association of American Cemetery Superintendents. But Smith, like Cothran, makes little use of the newspapers that let Giguere explore more closely dissemination, reception, and controversy.

Smith misdated the first attempts to regulate behavior and saw $5 as a "stiff" penalty (51), a tenth of some Giguere cites. She demonstrates how regulation evolved as a dialogue between patrons and administrators. In addressing class-based behavioral expectations respecting public space, she references extensive literature on theater audiences and promenade settings, as well as the early parks movement. She argues cogently that as "liminal space[s] between public and private" (93) rural cemeteries were both places to see and be seen and sites of grief and contemplation, with visitors taking their behavioral cues from their reasons for being there. Her sensitivity to nuance and command of the literature are couched in engaging prose.

Giguere presents examples from the Midwest and Pacific coast, but as an astute historian of the South, she highlights ways Southern rural cemeteries were distinctive. Far from naturalizing an inevitable proliferation, she probes reception, resistance, and modification. How women in Baltimore allied with a local newspaper in combatting a ban on unaccompanied females, the Virginia legislature refused to incorporate Hollywood Cemetery as too close to Richmond, and rural elites rebuffed suggestions that suburban cemeteries offered a more secure future for family burial plots than the home plantation. A chapter on the Civil War highlights tensions over interment and commemoration especially acute in Kentucky, a slave state within the Union recast in a Confederate mold by postwar Lost Cause ideology.

She closes with the rural cemetery's transition into the lawn park, pioneered in Cincinnati in the 1850s and pastorally beautiful rather than ruggedly picturesque. By the progressive era, family (and clergy) were marginalized as death care was "outsourced" to professionalizing undertakers and cemetery superintendents. The lawn park model embraced the industry and technology from which the rural cemetery had offered respite.

Bruce S. Elliott
Professor Emeritus (History)
Carleton University, Ottawa, Canada

Isaac Shearn and Elgin Klugh, eds.
A Place for Memory: Baltimore's Historic Laurel Cemetery.

Rowman & Littlefield, 2023. 220 pp.
ISBN-13: 978–1538156131.

The story of Laurel Cemetery, a historic African American cemetery in Baltimore that was demolished in 1958 and replaced by a shopping mall, is a tragically familiar one, proving that Mark Twain was right that while history does not repeat itself, it often rhymes.

When Laurel Cemetery was incorporated in 1852, Maryland law precluded African Americans from incorporating institutions like cemeteries. Consequently, the incorporators and subsequent owners were white, disconnecting its ownership from its constituency from the very start. Evidence suggests that it was still active into the 1940s, although the space was compromised as early as 1931 when a gas station opened on part of the grounds. Descendants of people buried there first learned about the cemetery's imminent demise when bulldozers arrived at the site and a local funeral director started removing bodies to be relocated. Despite efforts, the work proceeded. The records for the cemetery are lost, so no one knows—even now—just how many people were interred there. This volume documents not only the history of this cemetery, but also the important archaeological and archival work to document it and the community activism to recognize and mark it. Sadly, Black cemeteries have disappeared in numerous cities with little trace; the great importance of this volume is both its comprehensive discussion of the history of Laurel Cemetery and its people and in providing a road map for other communities seeking to place such sites back into the historical memory.

The book's chapters, written by eight different authors, are broken into two parts. The first examines its history: origins, place in the Civil War and role as a national cemetery for "Colored Troops," prominent people and their activism, and decline. The second provides a valuable primer on documenting a seemingly undocumented burial ground. Ronald Castanzo's chapter on public archeology traces efforts to identify extant burial plots at the shopping center's meager green spaces and includes excellent discussions of technology and techniques for such research. Similarly, Glenn Blackwell points to ways to document burials, albeit painstakingly, through public records like death certificates, suggesting that the number of burials at Laurel Cemetery is even higher than the 18,715 already documented. Blackwell also gives invaluable insights into the historical African American community in Baltimore through the data collected from death certificates including mortality ages (47 percent of deaths came before age five, for example), occupations, and demographic shifts through last-known addresses.

A Place for Memory has two minor shortcomings, neither of which are the editors' fault. It's not an inexpensive book, unfortunately, so may not reach the wide readership it deserves. And the photos, which are valuable and interesting, would benefit from higher quality printing. Happily, the Laurel Cemetery Memorial Project website offers high quality versions of these images and many more.

Jeffrey Smith
Professor Emeritus
Lindenwood University

Hannah Malone. ***Architecture, Death and Nationhood: Monumental Cemeteries of Nineteenth-Century Italy.***

Routledge, 2017. xvi + 262 pp. ISBN 978-1-4724-4681-7.

Hannah Malone's *Architecture, Death, and Nationhood: Monumental Cemeteries of Nineteenth-Century Italy* is, simply put, a remarkable book. In the first scholarly English-language study of Italy's grandiose monumental cemeteries, Malone provides deep insight into burial grounds that were unlike any others in the world. Italy's monumental cemeteries feature vast, geometrically designed cores, incomparable sculpture and architecture, and massive gateways. Initiated primarily in Italy's north and central regions, the earliest responded to the Napoleonic edict of 1806–09 that forbade burial within city walls while much of Italy was under French rule. Malone uses a microhistorical and case study approach to introduce readers to the features that distinguish each cemetery along with a macrohistorical treatment of the larger forces transforming the nation and its cemeteries.

Malone gives equal weight to the political, social, and cultural contexts that shaped the monumental cemeteries. Some will remind readers of changing burial practices in nineteenth-century France, England, and the United States. Romantic perceptions of death, the Enlightenment emphasis on individual dignity, tourism, hygienic concerns, and the cemeteries' suburbanization all played a role. Others are specific to Italy. Politically, Italy was "disturbed ground" (203), beginning with Austrian and French occupations; the Restoration (1814–15); the *Risorgimento,* or struggle for unification (1815–60s); and unification itself, completed in 1870. Each era is reflected in changes in the design of cemeteries and their tombs and architecture, making them an essential resource for understanding the evolving nation.

Socially, Italy experienced the rise of the middle class to positions of wealth and power. "The role of cemeteries," Malone writes, "was enhanced as burial was elevated to be a medium of expression and status within the social practices of the middle classes" (2). The newly wealthy built tombs that lined the cloisters and walkways, often featuring imaginative sculpture encouraged by the Romantic desire to evoke emotion and the realist style. Sculpture of figures in contemporary dress astonish in their faithfulness to the tiniest details. Another social factor was the clergy's declining power as municipalities took control of the cemeteries. Cremation, first employed in 1876, was a particular struggle between the Catholic Church and the progressives who promoted its practical value. Crematoria, a new type of architectural structure, were often traditional in form to make the controversial practice more acceptable.

Culturally, Italy witnessed significant shifts in style across the century encouraged by social and political change. The earliest monumental cemeteries embraced neoclassicism, with gateways and chapels emulating the Roman Pantheon. Surprisingly, unification in the 1860s led to a rejection of neoclassicism for medievalism that was viewed as more Italian, and more regional, best embodied by the Lombard-Romanesque design of Milan Monumental Cemetery's entry complex.

The book starts not with the Napoleonic edict but the reform efforts that preceded it, beginning in 1740, invigorated by Enlightenment ideas. Most interesting are the circumstances that revise our understanding of cemetery history. It was not France that first realized dramatic burial reform but Italy, with innovations like the Cemetery of the Three Hundred and Sixty-Six Graves, founded in 1762 in Naples, in which a hole for each day accommodated the poor who died on that day, and the suburban *fopponi* (large pits) of Milan dating to 1786. A second eighteenth-century influence was the "paper projects" produced by French and Italian academies, unrealized proposals for utopian burial grounds dedicated to meritocracy and the reform of social differences.

Chapter two defines the monumental cemetery as a unique architectural type. The emphasis on monumental architecture and geometric ground plans, along with a fascinating range of factors Malone details such as Catholic aversion to in-ground burial, resulted in the rejection of the nineteenth century's leading design innovation, the garden cemetery. What appealed to reformers in France, England, and the United States had little impact on Italy's new cemeteries, with only a few important exceptions at Staglieno in Genoa, Verano in Rome, and Poggioreale in Naples, which later added wooded, irregular plans. New attitudes toward death and commemoration encouraged by romanticism and patriotism reflected "a network of cultural and political forces that characterized the new nation state" (49).

Nineteenth-century Italy experienced a paroxysm as fragmented and often antagonistic states struggled to form a unified country. In chapter three, Malone argues most convincingly about the impact of the

Risorgimento on the cemeteries and the cemeteries on the Risorgimento. As states negotiated local, regional, and national patriotism, the cemeteries became both embodiments of local power and "key pedagogical instruments in the project to nationalise the Italian population" (105). A result of war and unification was the introduction of the *famedio* (temple of fame), significant structures or areas in the cemeteries that heroized worthy citizens, patriots, and the war dead, demonstrating the role that shared memory of the dead played in forming a national identity.

The fourth chapter concentrates on one of Malone's primary objectives, to "expose how architecture is shaped by sociopolitical and cultural conditions" (2), with examination of the cemeteries' architectural styles and a thorough consideration of meanings "rooted in history and the collective memory" (151). Here Malone digs deeply into the initial embrace of neoclassicism, creating a uniformity of design that reflected the push for unification. As noted, with unification, neoclassicism was rejected for medievalism and eclecticism that allowed cities to celebrate their roots and extended to tomb and monument design, which became increasingly individualized and magnificent.

Malone expertly teases out how myriad forces formed the cemeteries and how the cemeteries came to embody "a complex web of values" (205). The book concludes with a useful catalogue of one-page summaries of twenty-five cemeteries. Malone's bibliography reveals an astounding range of sources, including archival materials from the cities that house the cemeteries, interdisciplinary secondary sources, and popular ephemera like guidebooks. The book is illustrated with crisp black and white photographs and architectural drawings. It leaves no question that Italy's cemeteries deserve the same level of attention as those of France, England, and the United States. As Malone concludes, "The significance of the Italian cemeteries can be measured by the extent to which the living awarded meaning to the architecture of the dead" (202).

Elisabeth L. Roark
Professor of Art History
Chatham University

The Year's Work in Cemetery and Gravestone Studies

An International Bibliography

Compiled by Simon M. Braune

This annual feature of *Markers,* inaugurated in 1995, is intended to serve as an ongoing, working bibliography of pertinent scholarship in the interdisciplinary field of cemetery and gravemarker studies, including relevant works dealing with cenotaphs, public monuments, and/or memorials. With significant exceptions, since 2004, it has, for the most part, restricted itself to English-language works in the modern era (i.e., post-1500), consisting of books, scholarly articles, and theses and dissertations. Where possible, we have also included the digital object identifier (doi), which can be used to locate the resource online.

Excluded from the bibliography are conference presentations, audiovisual materials, newspaper articles, book reviews, items in trade and popular magazines, compilations of gravemarker inscriptions, and a number of nonscholarly items of varying sorts. Also not included are articles found in *Markers* or in the *AGS Quarterly.* This year's bibliography features materials primarily published from July 2024 through July 2025. The editor invites authors who have published relevant scholarship in 2025 through July 2026 to submit bibliographic entries to agsmarkers@gmail.com.

Simon Michael Braune is an independent scholar. He holds an MLS from Indiana University and an MA in Near Eastern languages and civilizations from the University of Chicago.

BOOKS, MONOGRAPHS, AND PAMPHLETS

Bielawski, Krzysztof. *The Destruction of Jewish Cemeteries in Poland.* Translated by Richard Bialey. Academic Studies Press, 2024. https://doi.org/10.1515/9798887195704-005.

Brandis, Veronika, Jan L. De Jong, and Robert Seidel, eds. *Funerary Inscriptions in Early Modern Europe.* Brill, 2025. https://doi.org/10.1163/9789004711709.

Brataas, Kjell. *Disaster Memorials and Monuments: History, Context and Practice from Around the World.* Routledge, 2024. https://doi.org/10.4324/9781003406167.

Brown, Ian W. *Confessions of a Cemeterian.* Borgo Publishing, 2024.

Ferri, Jessica. *Buried Hollywoodland: The Cemeteries of Los Angeles.* Fonthill Media, 2025.

Fisher, John. *Sacred Space and Anglo-Turkish Relations: The Politics of British Churches, Cemeteries, and War Graves in Turkey, 1825 to 1976.* Bloomsbury, 2024. https://doi.org/10.5040/9780755654659.

Gamberi, Valentina, and Chiara Calzana, eds. *Haunting Ruins: Ethnographies of Ruination and Decay.* Berghahn Books, 2025. https://doi.org/10.2307//jj.18163675.

Grady, Tim. *Burying the Enemy: The Story of Those Who Cared for the Dead in Two World Wars.* Yale University Press, 2025. https://doi.org/10.2307//jj.26193498.

Griffiths-Jones, A. J. *Buried Alive: A History of Premature Burials and Accidental Interments.* Pen & Sword Books, 2025.

Hansen-Glucklich, Jennifer. *German Memorials, Motifs, and Meanings: A Cultural History in Bronze, Wood, and Stone.* University of Massachusetts Press, 2025. https://doi.org/10.2307//jj.20036885.

Jameson, John H., Sherene Baugher, and Richard Veit, eds. *Monuments and Memory: Archaeological Perspectives on Commemoration.* University Press of Florida, 2025. https://doi.org/10.5744/florida/9780813079233.001.0001.

Lacy, Robyn S. *Daisy Wheel, Hexfoil, Hexafoil, Rosette: Protective Marks in Gravestone Art.* Berghahn Books, 2024. https://doi.org/10.3167/9781805396635.

Lilly, Carol S. *Death and Burial in Socialist Yugoslavia: The Politicization of Cemeteries and Ethnic Conflict in the Balkans.* Bloomsbury, 2024. https://doi.org/10.5040/9781350285859.

Lloveras, Lluís, Carme Rissech, Jordi Nadal, and Philip Banks, eds. *Reconstructing Past Monastic Life: Volume 1: Bioarchaeology, Life and Death: New Trends from Archaeological, Bioanthropological, and Documentary Perspectives.* Oxbow Books, 2025. https://doi.org/10.2307//jj.30297090.

Lye, Kit Ying, and Terence Heng, eds. *Death and the Afterlife: Multidisciplinary Perspectives from a Global City.* Taylor & Francis, 2024. https://doi.org/10.4324/9781003344858.

Macsotay, Tomas, and Nausikaä El-Mecky, eds. *Toppling Things as Memorial Contestation: Spectacle and Affect of Monument Removal.* Brill, 2025. https://doi.org/10.1163/9789004712645.

Nakano, Yoshiko, and Georgina Challen. *Meiji Graves in Happy Valley: Stories of Early Japanese Residents in Hong Kong.* Hong Kong University Press, 2025. https://doi.org/10.2307//jj.24653163.

Oakley, Jackie. *A Field Guide to the Vacant Chair Gravestone in Central Illinois: The Myths, the Practices, and Beyond.* Cheep Cheep Productions, 2024.

Parisot, Eric, David McAllister, and Xavier Aldana Reyes, eds. *Graveyard Gothic.* Manchester University Press, 2024. https://doi.org/10.7765/9781526166326.

Peterson, Pam Matthias. *A Guide to Historic Burial Grounds of Marblehead.* Arcadia Publishing, 2025.

Sarmiento, Ignacio. *Specters of War: The Battle of Mourning in Postconflict Central America.* University of Arizona Press, 2025. https://doi.org/10.2307/jj.24900058.

Seidemann, Ryan M. *Cemetery Protections in Urban Environments: Archaeology, Preservation, and the Law.* University Press of Florida, 2025. https://doi.org/10.5744/9781683405108.

Spears, Timothy B. *America's National Cemeteries: A Meditation on History, Memory, and Place.* University of Alabama Press, 2025. https://doi.org/10.2307//jj.30346976.

Srodecki, Paul, and Daria Kozlova, eds. *War and Remembrance II: World War II and the Holocaust Between Tabooization and Competing Narratives in Post-Socialist Europe.* Brill, 2025. https://doi.org/10.30965/9783657797813.

Woodthorpe, Kate, Helen Frisby, and Bethan Michael-Fox, eds. *Death and Institutions: Processes, Places, and the Past.* Bristol University Press, 2025. https://doi.org/10.2307//jj.18323750.

SCHOLARLY JOURNAL ARTICLES AND EDITED COLLECTIONS

Alexander, Kaylee P. "After Nadar: The Popularization of the Paris Catacombs in Print." *Dix-Neuf* 29 (2025): 1–21. https://doi.org/10.1080/14787318.2024.2443299.

Alexander, Kristen, and Kate Ariotti. "'Laid to Rest in Australian Soil': The Legacies of Repatriation Policy Change During the Vietnam War." *Australian Journal of Politics & History* 71, no. 3 (2025): 440–59. https://doi.org/10.1111/Ajph.13044.

Alvarado, Roxana. "Pandemic Antigones: The Role of Women in Shaping Funeral Practices in Chile." *Death Studies* 49, no. 10 (2025): 1306–15. https://doi.org/10.1080/07481187.2025.2454493.

Aytemiz Karslı, Pelin. "Visual Narratives of Islamic Funeral Practices in the Late Ottoman Empire and Early Turkish Republic." *Visual Anthropology* 37, no. 5 (2025): 438–69. https://doi.org/10.1080/08949468.2024.2409592.

Bateman, Roger. "Islamic Life and Death in Australia, after 1890: The Archaeology of Cameleer Burials." *Australian Archaeology* 91, no. 1 (2025): 47–64. https://doi.org/10.1080/03122417.2024.2416737.

Bazhenova, Hanna. "First World War Memorialization in Ukrainian Lands (Late 1910s to 1930s)." In *The Great War and the Anthropocene,* edited by Kerstin S. Jobst, Oksana Nagornaia, and Kerstin von Lingen. Brill, 2024. https://doi.org/10.1163/9789004711815_015.

Berger, Andreas. "Innovating The Aesthetics of Hebrew: Jewish Headstones in Basel and Humanist Epitaph Writing." *The Sixteenth Century Journal* 56, no. 1 (2025): 3–22. https://doi.org/10.1086/733576.

Blackburn, Kevin. "Cityscape and Memoryscape: The Cold War and Monuments of Commemoration in Singapore." In *The Cityscapes of Taipei, Hong Kong, and Singapore During the Cold War,* edited by Tze-Ki Hon and Ying-Kit Chan. Amsterdam University Press, 2025. https://doi.org/10.2307//jj.26844244.14.

Bugnon, Pascale. "Heritagization of an Islamic Site in China: The Mausoleum of Saʿd Ibn Abī Waqqāṣ in Guangzhou." *Journal of Chinese Religions* 53, no. 1 (2025): 75–99. https://doi.org/10.1353/jcr.2025.a960753.

Cashman, Ray. "What's Old Is New Again: Willow Coffins, Tradition, and Revival in Ireland Today." *New Hibernia Review* 29, no. 1 (2025): 21–41. https://dx.doi.org/10.1353/nhr.2025.a961107.

Dema, Eva. "'Sacred to The Memory': Thomas Hardy's Tombstones." *Review of English Studies* 75, no. 320 (2024): 280–98. https://doi.org/10.1093/Res/Hgae028.

Dugnoille, Julien. "'Death Is Nothing at All': A More-Than-Human Economy of Salvation in French Animal Cemeteries." *Society & Animals* (Published online 2025). https://doi.org/10.1163/15685306-Bja10219.

Duró, Ágota, and David Palmer. "Japan's Forgotten Korean Forced Laborers: The Search for Hidden Wartime Graves in Hokkaido." *International Labor and Working-Class History* 106 (October 2024): 311–30. https://doi.org/10.1017/S0147547924000048.

Earle, Julia E. "Tombs as Evidence of Religious Diversity in the Sacred Valley, Peru (ca. AD 1000–1532)." *Latin American Antiquity* (Published online 2025): 1–23. https://doi.org/10.1017/laq.2024.28.

Fan, Ka-Wai. "Chinese Diaspora Cemeteries: A Review." *Journal of Chinese Overseas* 21, no. 1 (2025): 67–94. https://doi.org/10.1163/17932548-12341525.

Farrow, Thomas J. "Death, Burial, and Commemoration in 19th- and Early-20th Century British 'Lunatic Asylum' and 'Mental Hospital' Cemeteries," *European Journal for the History of Medicine and Health* 81, no. 2 (2024): 266–304. https://doi.org/10.1163/26667711-20240015.

Grupa, Dawid. "Silk Textiles in Funerary Liturgical Garments in Poland (Seventeenth to Nineteenth Centuries)." In *Funerary Textiles in Situ: Towards A Better Method for The Study of Textile-Related Burial Practices,* edited by Elsa Yvanez and Magdalena M. Wozniak. Springer, Cham, 2025. https://doi.org/10.1007/978-3-031-69461-5_4.

Henderson, Gretchen Ernster. "The Missing Wreath: On JFK's Grave & Mrs. Mellon's Maquette." *Ploughshares* 50, no. 3 (2024): 52–100. https://doi.org/10.1353/plo.2024.a939127.

Holleran, Samuel. "Library of Stone: Cemeteries, Storytelling, and the Preservation of Urban Infrastructures of Death and Mourning." *Footprint* 18, no. 1 (2024): 41–54. https://doi.org/10.59490/Footprint.18.1.6956.

Islam, Quazi Tahsinul, Shabab Islam, and Ahmed I. Kabir. "Green Departures: The Loop Coffins Revolution in Sustainable Death Care." In *Sage Business Cases*. Sage Publications, 2025. https://doi.org/10.4135/9781071968888.

Johnson, Brian, and Richard Wittmann. "Funerary Heritage of the Grand Champs Des Morts: Evidence of Istanbul's Communal Diversity in Feriköy." In *Constantinople Through the Ages*, edited by Diedrik Burgersdijk, Fokke Gerritsen, and Willemjin Waal. Brill, 2024. https://doi.org/10.1163/9789004710986_013.

Joyce, Charles T. "'Died at Gettysburg!' No Prouder Epitaph Need Any Man Covet.": The Tragedy of Capt. Richard Wistar Davids of the 118th Pennsylvania Infantry." *Military Images* 43, no. 3 (2025): 50–59.

Khetrapal, Neha. "Memorials and Memory: A Material Turn." In *Memory Studies in India*, edited by Avishek Parui and Merin Simi Raj. Brill, 2025. https://doi.org/10.1163/9789004722514_004.bra.

Knighton, Tess. "Burying the Bones: Mapping the Sounds and Spaces of the Confraternity of the Verge Maria Dels Desamparats in Early Modern Barcelona." In *Listening to Confraternities*, edited by Tess Knighton. Brill, 2024. https://doi.org/10.1163/9789004702776_020.

Krishna, Aswathy. "Remembering Bhima Koregaon: Contesting Historical Memories Around Memorial Buildings." In *Memory Studies in India*, edited by Avishek Parui and Merin Simi Raj. Brill, 2025. https://doi.org/10.1163/9789004722514_003.

Lipkin, Sanna. "Research on Post-Medieval Funerary Attire: Ethics, Challenges, and Successful Methods for Studying Coffin Textiles Found Below Finnish Church Floors." In *Funerary Textiles in Situ: Towards A Better Method for The Study of Textile-Related Burial Practices*, edited by Elsa Yvanez and Magdalena M. Wozniak. Springer, Cham, 2025. https://doi.org/10.1007/978-3-031-69461-5_5.

Montón-Subías, Sandra, and Laura Trelliso Carreño. "The Colonization of Death in the Mariana Islands and the Cemetery of San Dionisio at Humåtak, Guåhan." *International Journal of Historical Archaeology* 29 (September 2025): 1–26. https://doi.org/10.1007/s10761-024-00763-5.

Muller, Stephen. "Representations of Childness: The Memorialisation of Children in the Australian Cemetery 1836–2018." *Mortality* 29, no. 3 (2024): 531–53. https://doi.org/10.1080/13576275.2023.2192341.

Murphy, Damian. "Costello Mortuary Chapel: Carrick-On-Shannon, Co. Leitrim." *History Ireland* 32, no. 5 (2024): 31–34. https://www.jstor.org/stable/e27390552.

Nagar, Yossi, Noé David Michael, Oren Shmueli, and Elena Kogan-Zehavi. "A Mother and Child Reunion? An Unusual Ottoman-Period Bedouin Pit Grave at Rahat, the Northern Negev." *'Atiqot* 117 (2025): 295–310. https://www.jstor.org/stable/e27389113.

Nwoko, Kenneth Chukwuemeka. "Graveyards, Epitaphs, and Burial Traditions in Colonial Lagos, 1861–1960." *Canadian Journal of African Studies/Revue Canadienne Des Études Africaines* 59, no. 3 (March 2025): 1–21. https://doi.org/10.1080/00083968.2024.2446766.

O'Brien, Dan. "The Undertakers of Eighteenth-Century Bath." In *Bath and Beyond: The Social and Cultural World of the Georgian Assembly Room*, edited by Hillary Burlock, Robin Eagles, and Tatjana LeBoff. Routledge, 2025. https://doi.org/10.4324/9781003393856.

O'Flaherty, Ronan, Michael Brazzill, James Barry, and Kieran Craven. "Looking for A Stony Place." *Archaeology Ireland* 38, no. 3 (2024): 22–25. https://www.jstor.org/stable/27391013.

Öztürk, Ali Osman, and Meral Ozan. "'May He/She Rest in Lights': Araştırma Makalesi/Research Article Reflection on Wishes in Funerary Folklore." *Türk Folklor Araştırmaları Derneği Dergisi* 371 (2025): 19–37. https://doi.org/10.61620/Tfa.66.

Perani, Mauro. "The 1625 Trial Against The 'Heretical' Epitaphs in Jewish Cemetery of Ancona." In *The Many Faces of Early Modern Italian Jewry: Religious, Cultural, and Social Identities*, edited by Martin Borýsek and Davide Liberatoscioli. De Gruyter, 2024. https://doi.org/10.1515/9783111049151-010.

Ruszała, Kamil. "Conceptualizing the Post-Battle Landscape: The First World War Military Cemeteries and Monuments in Galicia." In *The Great War and the Anthropocene*, edited by Kerstin S. Jobst, Oksana Nagornaia, and Kerstin von Lingen. Brill, 2024. https://doi.org/10.1163/9789004711815_014.

Ryko, Anastasiia. "Funeral Rites in The Russian-Belarusian Borderland: Traditions and Innovations." *Chinese Journal of Slavic Studies* 5, no. 1 (2025): 114–29. https://doi.org/10.1515/Cjss-2025-0001.

Salguero Montaño, Óscar. "Islamic Thought, Funerary Space and Urban Policies: The Case of Madrid." *Journal of Muslims in Europe* 13, no. 3 (2024): 352–64. https://doi.org/10.1163/22117954-Bja10108.

Scott, Grant F. "Memorialising Keats: Severn, Headstones and *Hyperion*." *Romanticism* 30, no. 2 (2024): 180–200. https://doi.org/10.3366/rom.2024.0646.

Shay, Talia. "Your Loved One Can't Rest Near Mine: The Materiality of a Contemporary Immigrants' Cemetery." *Archaeologies* 21 (June 2025): 1–27. https://doi.org/10.1007/s11759-025-09531-1.

Shi, Lihong. "My Child's Home: Parental Grief at a Chinese Cemetery." *Death Studies* 49, no. 10 (2024): 1353–62. https://doi.org/10.1080/07481187.2024.2435931.

Taxel, Itamar, Roy Marom, and Yossi Nagar. "An Infant Jar Burial from Zarnūqa: Muslim Funerary Practices and Migrant Communities in Late

Ottoman Palestine." *'Atiqot* 117 (2025): 269–94. https://doi.org/10.70967/2948-040X.2262.

Vagni, Juan José, and Julia Solana Jáuregui. "The 1910 Centenary Plaque: The Memory and Heritage of Arab Communities in Córdoba, Argentina." In *Art and Politics Between the Arab World and Latin America*, edited by Laure Guirguis and Maru Pabon. Brill, 2025. https://doi.org/10.1163/9789004724815_004.

DISSERTATIONS AND THESES

Bilchak, Rachel Victoria. "Gravestone Studies of Imperial County: Formal-Temporal Trends in Rural Cemetery Markings." Master's thesis, San Diego State University, 2025.

Boyle, Colleen. "Minding Your Feet: An Examination of Cemetery Recordation and Analysis Through Geospatial Documentation in Fairfax County, Virginia." Master's thesis, University of Maryland, College Park, 2024. https://doi.org/10.13016/ot0t-6izk.

Buchert, Martha Clare. "'For There is Hope of a Tree . . .': A Study of Two Historic African American Cemeteries in Pope County, Illinois." Master's thesis, Southern Illinois University Carbondale, 2025. https://opensiuc.lib.siu.edu/theses/3344/.

Byron, Cameron. "Territories and Terrains of Death and Burial: Governing Volumes, Materialities, and Everyday Geopolitical Bodies across Wirral Cemeteries." PhD diss., University of Liverpool, 2024. https://doi.org/10.17638/03184769.

Da Cunha, Paulo Vítor Mendes. "Beyond the Headstones: A Geophysical Study of the Garrison Hill Cemetery Relocation." Master's thesis, Southern Illinois University Carbondale, 2025. https://www.proquest.com/openview/9f5a6a70d4d8b49e0a9738673eb82f7e/1.pdf?pq-origsite=gscholar&cbl=18750&diss=y.

Furney, Anna. "Victorian Cemeteries: How Missouri Follows Changes and Trends in Remembering the Dead." Master's thesis, University of Central Missouri, 2024.

Glantz, Jillian. "Reclaiming Restlawn: A Historic Black Cemetery in Edinburg, Texas, 1928–Present." Master's thesis, Texas A&M University, 2024. https://hdl.handle.net/1969.1/1593799.

Hallenbeck, Jenna. "Mortuary Culture and Social Memory at the Agua Mansa Pioneer Cemetery." Master's thesis, California State University, Northridge, 2025. http://hdl.handle.net/20.500.12680/5m60r250f.

Hammerschmidt, Tori Lee. "Eternal Rest Disrupted: Techniques for Locating Impermanent Graves of Lost Institutional Cemeteries: State Farm Cemetery of Cranston Rhode Island." Master's thesis, University of Maryland, College Park, 2025. https://doi.org/10.13016/lovl-elp0.

Kwun, Namhi. "Burning S(e)oul: A Body for Cremation." PhD diss., Massachusetts Institute of Technology, 2025. https://hdl.handle.net/1721.1/162072.

McMillan, Alessandra Jordyn. "Death and Heritage: An Archaeological Analysis of the Differential Treatment of Two Historic Burial Grounds in Ferryland, Newfoundland." Master's thesis, Memorial University of Newfoundland, 2024. https://doi.org/10.17615/e663-by27.

Zurek-Ost, Andrea M. "Mobility and Burial Along the Way of Saint James: Embodiment and Ephemerality at the Silo of Charlemagne." PhD diss., University of North Carolina at Chapel Hill, 2025. https://doi.org/10.17615/e663-by27.